T0115016

Navigating the Rapids and the Waves of Life

10 Lessons for Managing Emotions for Success

MAVIS MAZHURA

BALBOA.
PRESS
A DIVISION OF HAY HOUSE

Balboa Press books may be ordered through booksellers or by contacting:

Balboa Press
A Division of Hay House
1663 Liberty Drive
Bloomington, IN 47403
www.balboapress.com
1 (877) 407-4847

Because of the dynamic nature of the Internet, any web addresses or links contained in this book may have changed since publication and may no longer be valid. The views expressed in this work are solely those of the author and do not necessarily reflect the views of the publisher, and the publisher hereby disclaims any responsibility for them.

The author of this book does not dispense medical advice or prescribe the use of any technique as a form of treatment for physical, emotional, or medical problems without the advice of a physician, either directly or indirectly. The intent of the author is only to offer information of a general nature to help you in your quest for emotional and spiritual well-being. In the event you use any of the information in this book for yourself, which is your constitutional right, the author and the publisher assume no responsibility for your actions.

Any people depicted in stock imagery provided by Thinkstock are models, and such images are being used for illustrative purposes only.
Certain stock imagery © Thinkstock.

Printed in the United States of America.

ISBN: 978-1-4525-2079-7 (sc)
ISBN: 978-1-4525-2081-0 (hc)
ISBN: 978-1-4525-2080-3 (e)

Library of Congress Control Number: 2014915163

Balboa Press rev. date: 08/26/2014

Navigating the Rapids and the Waves of Life

10 Lessons for Managing Emotions for Success

is dedicated to hundreds of souls who have shared their emotional journeys with me on my programs, seminars, live classes, emails and articles. My friends, my family, my siblings and my business partners, all are my teachers, guiding me to become the best I can be. They love, challenge, oppose and push me to limits, but all with the aim to teach me to become better than I was yesterday.

This book is dedicated to my husband Prince and our 2 boys, Tadi and Maka. Managing emotions for success will create the best possible relationships we can have as a family. They teach me every day to manage my emotions for success.

We all get messed up by emotion' sometimes when we fail to manage them and they get the better part of us. This book is dedicated to you.

Contents

Preface

Greetings. My name is Mavis Mazhura

This may be our first meeting, or we may have met at one of training seminars over the years.

As a speaker, teacher, trainer, coach and business owner, I have worked with hundreds of people helping them to reach their full potential in work performance, relationships, finances, mental and spiritual well-being.

All the interaction I have had with people who improve their lives and achieve success in any area of the life, Managing Emotions for Success became a vital tool to move from point A to point B. While I teach I must acknowledge that I am a student of this topic myself because every interaction has left me with something new about the power of emotions to either move you forward or keep you stuck.

Stay tuned, be open-minded as you go through the book and do your best to go through all the activities. Take time to reflect and practice using the tools and techniques in this book and I promise you will find it worthwhile.

Let us begin the exploration!

Acknowledgements

I had a major struggle; I had a teacher's certificate
and realized for the first time in my life that I was
not an educated person. I was this person who had
gotten wonderful grades and knew nothing, who
had very few skills.

— Grace Llewellyn

This book represents the accumulative wisdom of many great
thinkers on the topic. It is a synthesis of my understanding on
this subject from what I have learnt from my great teachers some
of whom I have come across including Dr John Demartini, John
Maxwell, Dr Myles Munroe, Joshua Freedman, Francois Basili,
Tom Beasor, Bill Cropper, Bennie Naude and many others. Putting
this book together has helped to confirm that I am a student of
emotions, they teach me everyday and at this moment I see myself
as a lifetime student of this subject.

What I have achieved is a result of being taught and teaching
others to achieve their success is my contribution to humanity, the
universe and use of my gifts from God.

Joshua Freedman helped me to appreciate how emotional
intelligence can transform one's life going forward. I had a
question that lingered in my head though, how do I manage
unresolved emotions from my past as I often found them
disruptive or interfering with my present and future. Dr
Demartini's breakthrough experience course answered that

question. His course shifted my deep seated beliefs that I was holding onto, to justify my victim mentality and keep stuck. I literally got sick after the course because the false security of negative emotions that had formed my dysfunctional beliefs had been blown away. I realized that shift is possible, anyone can change but the role of a teacher cannot be downplayed in the process. I also learnt that emotions buried alive will never die, they are live wires that can spark an undesired reaction or behavior which can destroy relationships, influence one to make decisions that they may regret, cause set backs in any area of one's life.

As I interacted with others in my seminars I witnessed a lot of emotional pain and suffering mainly from past experiences and I began to ask myself, how do I help these people to be free, to release these negatively charged emotions that maybe holding them back. I came across Nick Ortner's Emotional Freedom Technique, but he was too far and Bennie Naude came to my rescue. I learnt a tool that is useful for clearing the body's energy system and releasing negative emotions.

While releasing emotions worked wonders I also realized that I had developed adaptive strategies over the years and you can call this my personality. I needed a tool that can help me become more aware of my tendencies, strengths and weaknesses. Tom Beasor came to my rescue and introduced me to the Strength Deployment Inventory, a personality tool that helps one understand how they behave when things are going well and when they are in conflict. This awareness helped me to develop personalized coaching sessions that helped me and others to discover deeply fixed, consistent, distinctive and personality patterns of thoughts, feelings and behaviors that effect one's performance, results and relationships.

Most of all, I want to thank my late sister Tendai Mujera (nee Mazhura) for instilling the value of hard work and the greatest source of all teaching. My sister and I defined significance differently which led to some of the battles we had but I love my sister deeply. And it is this process that has birthed this book. Thank you to my teachers.

Introduction

"What is "Navigating the Waves and the Rapids of Life, Managing Emotions for Success"?

Emotions can get in the way or can get you on the way
— Mavis Mazhura

Every day, we hear stories about road rage, suicide, terminal sicknesses, stress, failed relationships, bullying and some shocking like murder. But you also hear inspiring stories of people who survive tragedies, create a new product or create a solution to a problem. And I do not know if it is just me, but the negative stories seem to be escalating, or maybe we are just focusing more on the negative. And the question that you may also ask is what is going on in our world. Closely looking at all the stories you will realize that there is always something they all have in common: EMOTIONS. Our feelings are so powerful, they can create or destroy, they influence everything we do on a daily basis, either positive or negative, even when we are not aware. We feel all the time, so we always have emotions. activating or deactivating us. However, many of us have never been educated about emotions for us to understand them and to be able to manage them productively.

Using the metaphor of a river, its features such as the waves and currents to represent the continuous flow of emotions, this book's aim is to develop emotional literacy and give tools, techniques and reflective questions to understanding and managing emotions.

Can we manage EMOTIONS productively and create the results we want? The answer is YES. This book is designed to help you manage your emotions for success. It is not a quick fix but a process and also a continuous journey. When you embark on this journey you are joining many who are already students of emotions. Emotions teach you everyday by showing you opportunities or threats in your environment. As you enhance your understanding of emotions you will realise that they are messages, or information that we need to use to guide our actions with awareness instead of them taking us somewhere blind-folded.

Meet your new teacher, EMOTIONS and enjoy the learning!

Flow—The Natural State of Being

Feelings are much like waves. We can't stop them from coming, but we can choose which one to surf.
—Jonathan Mårtensson

We headed towards Jinja, Uganda, on a tour bus from Kampala, and we picked up some people along the way. I was going for river rafting, courtesy of Kelly McTavish Mungar, the executive director of Pearl of Africa Tours. She had attended our Emotional Intelligence course in Kampala that I facilitated, and she suggested river rafting for me.

Initially, I was not sure I wanted to go, but later on, I thought, *Why not?* I was clueless as to what river rafting was all about and had not even made an effort to search on the Internet or read about it. When we got to Jinja, we were given a briefing on the plan for the day and were given our kit, life jacket, helmet and a small breakfast. We got on the tour truck, and off to the river we went.

I felt like I was on my own, although in a group. What I mean is that I had not come with anyone; everyone there was with a partner, family, or a friend. I had no idea what to expect, given that I do not make friends easily. I had never been on a river raft. Interestingly, I cannot swim, and I was water phobic after a near-drowning experience, but I assumed the river rafting would be a leisurely, smooth sail along the river, where I could even take photos and do my work—I took a laptop and a camera in my handbag. I had no rafting literacy, but I was in for the adventure.

As we got to the river, we disembarked and gathered beside the river as the inflatable boats, safety boats, and paddles were being offloaded. To my amazement, I realized that my expectations were off the mark. I had to adjust to what was going on—the reality. We all had to wear our gear and get another briefing on procedures and safety precautions. All the electronics and valuables remained in the tour bus. We had about six guides. Doug, our main guide, explained the duration of the course and what we would encounter on the course. He suggested that we team up with people with similar experience and interests. Each team was then assigned an expert—a guide.

When joining up into raft groups, the guide asked whether one wanted to have a "crazy" or a "mellow" day. If we chose crazy, we would take the biggest rapids head-on and most likely flip over on at least three of them. Flipping over can be a little thrilling, and it really is phenomenally fun and exciting. If we chose mellow, we would try to avoid the biggest part of the rapids but still might flip once or twice. If we wanted an exciting day, he said, definitely try to avoid getting on a raft with anyone who wants mellow day, or we'd be looking longingly at the groups high-fiving each other after surviving another exhilarating flip.

The rapids started immediately with an eight-foot waterfall drop, and then there were about ten other rapids, three or four of which the guide said were class five. Each rapid had a name. I remember one class-five rapid called the Dutchman, where a Dutch man died. The class five represents the difficulty and is impossibly hard to navigate. Although their rating system is far too liberal, the waves on some of the rapids, where the water takes a big drop and then ramps back upward, are huge. There are long lulls of calm water between rapids, so we had a lot of downtime for snacks, swimming, bird watching, reflection, or just peace and quiet.

River rafting is experiencing the river and navigating the waves with either white water or the tranquil blue water. Our experience of emotions daily is like going on a river raft, where we have to navigate emotions that arise throughout the day due to the different circumstances we encounter and the changing environments. Like rafters along the river, we need skills to navigate the constant challenges and changes. Our operating and ever-changing environments can be likened to a river with class-one to class-five rapids, and each rapid will cause us to feel and think in a certain way, compelling us to act or behave in a certain way, and experiencing the different waves that come up as a result. We, therefore, need to have the expert skills of a kayaker to navigate thoughts and emotions and choose behaviors that get us in the direction we want. These skills of effectively navigating our emotions, thoughts and adopting ways of acting with maximum potential to enhance our lives is known as *emotional intelligence.*

The challenge with emotional intelligence is that, like Mavis going for a river raft without knowledge of what happens there, you may not have the necessary tools or knowledge to help you on your journey of life, yet every day you may act with ignorance or lack of knowledge. There was no module called river rafting in my entire eighteen years of schooling. Neither did my informal education, parents, siblings, or the community in which I lived teach me about it. For a lot of us, our formal and informal education systems did not provide the skills to navigate the changes and challenges we encounter *in life.* The good thing, though, is that we can still learn it on the way, at whatever stage we are in life, just as I experienced rafting the Nile River—without prior knowledge but with willingness to learn, change the status quo, practice, become better, and be flexible enough to let adventure in. I was a mediocre paddler, and I didn't know how to swim, but I was willing to learn. It is out of that adventure that I am able to reflect on the metaphor of a river as our daily life.

Having someone—expert guides who had knowledge of the river, who navigated it every day, knew the river like the backs of their hands, was willing to share what they know—made it easier. Our guides knew the history of the river, its development, structure and the impact this would have on our experience for that day. We all have gone through different experiences in life that have shaped the people that we are today, and that also impacts the way we experience life today, through our thoughts, feelings, and behaviors. Having this self-knowledge on how these experiences condition the people that we are or have become helps us to manage our interactions with others. This also helps to check if we are responding to what is happening or to what has happened.

At the end of the river raft, we had accomplished our mission for that day, and we were happy and looking forward to days ahead. Similarly, what we experience should not get us stuck. We need to keep moving ahead—that is, keep our natural state of being flowing.

The key lessons I took from the river raft that I believe are essential to learning and applying emotional intelligence in our lives for overall success are as follows:

> **Develop self- knowledge**
> **Stay present.**
> **Don't give power to external conditions.**
> **Adapt purposely.**
> **Have some tools and options.**
> **Team up with people who have created or are creating the results that you want.**
> **Don't flow back on yourself. Get out of obstructions as soon as possible. Your whole life still awaits you.**
> **Recharge.**
> **Flow on purpose and live.**
> **Celebrate at the *unsung hero* inside you.**

These key lessons will be explored throughout this book to demonstrate how they can assist you to develop or enhance your emotional intelligence. Emotional intelligence is an essential life skill that can transform your life, relationships, and performance at work and in life.

We all know, as human beings, that we do not do anything that has no benefit for us. You could ask yourself, *What is emotional intelligence, and what is the point?* Effectively navigating emotions will give you some of the following benefits:

Flow and Success

Emotions either get in the way or get you on the way. When you are flowing forward, you are on your way. Flow is our default state of being. Given that the greater percentage of our body is water, we are created to flow. About 60 percent of human body is water in adults, which means we are literally flowing most of the time even though we look solid. However, some life experiences disrupt the flow process. Emotional stress is regarded as the biggest killer of our times. Negative emotions, if not managed well, can be dangerous as they impact on our behavior and channel negative energy in the key areas of our lives, including finances, relationships, work life, physical health, mental health, and spiritual life. Our emotions are the continuous waves and undercurrents that enable us to flow, but in some instances, when we hold on to them, suppress or repress them, or express them destructively, they disrupt the flow. In our flow state, we experience positively charged emotions and we keep moving forward, but when we stagnate, we experience negatively charged emotions and we are stuck. Flow enhances success, as it gives energy that can even uproot obstacles to success. Success means different things to different people. However, when we are able to direct emotions in the direction we want or that gives us the results we want, we improve our performance toward our desired goals and success is the ultimate.

Success is achieving your mission. Success can be your ability to influence others in leadership, forming and maintaining great relationships, attaining financial freedom, advancing in your career, or whatever your goal is. And all these result from your actions and inactions. Your actions or inactions are influenced by your emotions or how you feel. What drives behavior are emotions. Your ability to channel emotions effectively, coupled with other skills you have, such as your intellect, will result in success. Effectively channeling your emotions in pursuit of your goals also enhances *flow*, which is your default state of being. For as long as you are alive, you need to keep moving or flowing, not stagnate or get stuck. Flow enhances well-being and happiness. Acting with intention in the present and with the outcome in mind is a key self-management skill that directs your efforts where you want to be.

Freedom

When you can do what you want when you want, with a purpose in mind, that is freedom. We all want some kind of freedom in key areas of our lives, such as finances, family, spiritual, mental, career, social, and physical. Emotions drive our actions or inactions, and this determines whether we are free or prisoners. Navigating emotions well will set us free and also help release any bondage we may have been carrying that is keeping our freedom captive. Self-mastery and self-knowledge are key emotional intelligence skills that enhance freedom.

Most people tend to punish themselves for things for which they are not responsible for, by taking ownership of the event or situation and/or taking identity in what has happened. They then get stressed and eventually die or live in bondage for the rest of their lives. Some of the emotions that keep people captive are regret, guilt, fear, jealousy, apathy and grief. Most of the time, when you experience these emotions, you are not in the present. You either are thinking of the past or the future. Some people never get over (or take a long time to get over) the loss of their loved ones, and they punish themselves, as if they have contributed to its happening. Yet it could be just a sequence of events, or something entirely out of their control, or just the law of the universe. Your dominant state, which is a combination of emotions you experience all the time, either make you free or enslaved. Are you free?

Wellness and Well-Being

Emotions can eat you up or make you eat. When emotions are suppressed or repressed, they become corrosive and toxic, corroding your body—that is, eating your body tissues. Some people are emotional eaters. When they feel unwell inside, due to negatively charged emotions, they soothe themselves with food, eating a lot and gaining weight. Then they feel unwell again due to how they look, which creates a vicious cycle. There are a series of vicious cycles in which many people are entangled. These include alcohol, prescription drugs (such as tranquilizers), excessive sex, compulsive behaviors, and so on, which give temporary relief but perpetuate feeling unwell inside.

Emotions can throw you off balance, and you experience a turbulence that can leave you feeling sick or unwell inside, stressed, depressed, angry, bitter, guilty, regretful, or anxious. Negatively charged emotions demoralize the body and take a toll on it. This opens the body to illness, instability of your overall well-being, and your ability to be happy. Dr. Caroline Leaf[1] indicates that research shows that 87 percent of illnesses can be attributed to our thoughts and emotional life, and only 13 percent to diet and environment. Studies have shown that emotions are the second biggest killer, after medicine, and that ignored, dismissed, repressed, or ventilated emotions can result in physical illness, such as cancer,

---

[1] Dr. Caroline Leaf, *Who Switched Off My Brain? Toxic, Thoughts, Emotions and Bodies* (2007).

arthritis, and other chronic illnesses. Regret and betrayal have also been linked to the cause of some of the fibroids.

Your ability to navigate emotions that arise from your life experiences and events will give you the resultant wellness and well-being. When you can navigate and manage your emotions, you can discipline yourself on what you eat or drink and make a commitment to habits that enhance wellness, like exercising. Chade Meng Tan[2] says happiness is our default state of being. Happiness enhances our flow state. Yet a lot of us struggle to return to or retain this default position. Many experience happiness as a visitor that comes once a year (like Christmas), once a month, or every Friday. Many people tend to energize negative emotions that we are supposed to release as soon as they arise. We make them bed and breakfast or give them permanent residence in our bodies. Some have literally moved in to steal our joy, and we are sadly unaware. Emotions, when expressed constructively, released, or transformed, enhance our wellness and well-being.

Great Performance

We all have the potential to function at a higher level by focusing our energy where we get results that serve us. Experiencing emotions means expending energy. A lot of us expend energy in worry, anxiety, and anger, without channeling that energy where we can get results. Like a car when we fill up our fuel tank, every mile we drive exhausts the fuel tank. Energy gets less and less. We also exhaust our energy levels on a daily basis by what we think, feel, and do. Our performance on anything requires energy, whether mental, physical, or emotional energy. We, however, carry on without thinking about where or how we are expending the energy. We have average performance, and we normalize it.

---

[2]   Chade Meng Tan, *Search Inside Yourself* (2012).

Joshua Freedman[3] says our performance on anything depends on how we feel about it. Emotions drive people, and people drive performance. Our ability to navigate emotions will determine what gets accomplished. Procrastination stems from how we feel about what needs to be done, hence time management is an emotional issue.

Creativity

The human mind has a tendency to oscillate between the past and the future and takes away attention from the present, which is where we can make impact, connections, and creativity. Creativity is just connecting things.

> *When you ask creative people how they did something, they feel a little guilty, because they didn't really do it; they just saw something.*
>
> —Steve Jobs

Seeing something requires awareness, a form of presence, being in the here and now. A clear mind is more creative. Creativity is hampered by only one way of looking at a problem. Creativity is enhanced by looking for options, keeping on making decisions, shying away from our patterns and schemas, and adopting an inclusive thinking to look at different ways of acting, being, feeling, and thinking. Emotional intelligence skills assist us in getting unstuck and being mindful—that is, paying attention to being purposeful.

Effective Communication

Your ability to communicate with yourself and others more directly, clearly, and honestly is key to getting the results you want.

---

[3]   Joshua Freedman, *At the Heart of Leadership* (2007).

Assertion is communicating purposefully, rather than reactively. High-achieving individuals and professionals use assertion to form positive and supportive relationships quickly in any setting. To communicate in ways that respect your rights and that also respect the rights of others, you have to regulate your emotions and manage impulses and internal states that interfere with effective communication. Have you ever listened to the voice that speaks to you about yourself? What does it say? We carry an ongoing conversation with ourselves about ourselves. The challenge with this is that whatever you say about yourself stands, as there is no one to defend you.

Self-assertion means communicating in a positive and constructive way, without being self-absorbed. Self-absorption is a hindrance to effective communication. Research shows that 90 percent of people spend 95 percent of their lives alone in their own heads. This means that the communication you have with others you actually have with yourself. To effectively communicate, you have to have the self-discipline to silence the internal chatter, so that you can pay attention fully to the other person or the issue at hand. This will enable you not to divert the story and issues and make it about you.

Great Relationships

Life coach, self help author and motivational speaker Robbins Anthony said that the quality of your life is measured by the quality of your relationships. When you have great supportive relationships at work, you can perform better, and supportive relationships at home will assist you in achieving all you want to achieve. Emotions can build or destroy a relationship. They lead to great or catastrophic decisions and influence your best and your worst behaviors. Your ability to manage emotions, to handle conflict without destroying relationships or making others feel unsafe around you, is a key attribute to building long-lasting relationships in an era where relationships are falling apart easily. When your relationships lack stability, you also are unstable.

The trend is that many of us are always starting or ending a relationship, either at work in our personal lives. Human beings are herd animals, created for companionship, and we constantly seek to relate. Emotional intelligence can assist us in building great relationships without self-sacrificing or coming across as arrogant, suspicious, smothering, or cold.

Problem Solving and Effective Decision Making

On a daily basis, we have to make decisions in dealing with challenges and solving the problems we encounter. When problems arise, so do our emotions, based on our perception and associated feelings of whatever is going on. We may encounter a fog of confusion and emotional entanglements. To problem solve, we have to know and understand how we are feeling and that our feelings have a huge impact on how we make the decisions we make.

Have you ever looked back at a problem you experienced and said to yourself, "I could have handled that better"? What happened for you to do what you did? Usually, when emotions take over, our rational-thinking abilities are suppressed and our ability to solve problems becomes narrowed. We react on our survival instinct level—fight or flight—even though what is happening is not necessarily a life-or-death issue. Emotional intelligence helps to identify these emotions and work with them or through them to respond to our situations, instead of reacting to them. It also helps us to check whether these feelings emanate from this particular problem or are linked to other problems that have occurred in the past, to our fears of the future, or our unmet needs. This will enable us to not let past or future emotions hijack the opportunity to solve this particular problem and focus on the current facts, not our schemas.

Recharge

It is amazing how we are so vigilant in ensuring that our cars are filled up, and we constantly check how we spend the fuel we put in it. Most human beings hardly make a conscious effort to check their own energy levels or how and where they spend their energy. We only realize when we are drained (lack of energy) or when we burn out that we have run out of energy. And the traditional thought then is to take a rest—sleep more to recuperate. Emotions are energy. Emotions can either energize you or de-energize you. And remember, there is no emotion without a thought, so your thoughts and emotions consume energy in your body but also create energy in your body. What do you spend your energy on? Are you aware of your thoughts and emotions throughout the day? How do you refuel or conserve your energy?

Will you do what it takes to learn how to recharge or have more energy? If your answer is yes, be open-minded to new ideas and be willing to practice new behaviors and transform your life. To get to where you are today, you have practiced a lot of things over and over again that have now become part of your being. You may even do some without thinking about it, because you have mastered the skill. The same goes with mastering emotional intelligence skills. We have to practice and undo some habits and patterns to let in new ways of acting or allow chosen behaviors that move us in the direction we want.

Think about it; have you ever been truly happy? How did you know you were happy? It affects every living cell in your body. But have you ever been sad? How did you know you were sad or where was that feeling of sadness? Negatively charged emotions are found in particular places in your body, like your neck or shoulders or a feeling of being heartbroken (we always joke that no heart ever breaks because we would be dead). When negatively charged emotions are not allowed to flow through and out, they find a place to settle in your body, disrupting the flow process and creating a form of a "dis-ease" in your body; for example, high blood pressure, heart disease, some of the cancers, and emotional bondage. When you are not flowing, it affects your performance to achieve your goals. Each time the waves of negative emotions seem bigger than you are, you can't accomplish much, or you end up engaging in behaviors that may give you temporary relief from what you are feeling, like alcohol or drug abuse; refusing sex or having too much sex with multiple partners; getting into the wrong relationship; or smoking. This does not fix the problem but instead might create other challenges and emotional upheavals later. The biggest challenge is curing this lack of emotional literacy to process the emotions and enhance flow.

Lesson 1

Develop Self-Knowledge

Developing self-knowledge is about self-awareness—knowing your tendencies, your strengths and weaknesses, and your purpose and accurately identifying how you feel and your triggers. How I wish we had such a manual in school for each one of us! We lead ourselves daily, and many of us are going to an unknown destination because we never take time to figure out who we are and where we are going. Many also struggle to lead or manage themselves because they do not know who they really are. They may even experience conflict with self between who they are and who they have been socialized to be.

Know Your Course

There are three things that are extremely hard: steel, a diamond, and to know oneself.
—Benjamin Franklin

The guide knew the route well and what to expect on the way. He had the ability to identify and name the different rapids scales of the river, their intensity, and the consequences of riding on them. He knew even the history of the river and could tell its story. The story had an effect on whether the present team would attempt certain areas or rapids that had caused fatalities or whether they had the skills to

1

navigate those white waters. Telling the story allowed those present to understand what lay before them and to choose their options.

The guide also knew the rules of the river. He indicated that if those who could not swim found themselves outside the boat for some reason, they should not try to stand; they should keep their legs flowing with the water, and someone would then be able to rescue them. If they tried to stand, they would definitely sink. Before we set off, we got on the boat and practiced what we would do along the way. The guide instructed us to paddle in different ways and asked us to remember to listen to *instructions* and paddle as he said. We also jumped out of the boat into the water individually and had a team member pull us back in.

The guide continued educating us about the sport, explaining that each raft required different navigation. Sometimes, we would make hard forward paddles or backward paddles. Our life jackets were on, and he educated us on how to be safe with them. River Nile makes a big statement with its story, its scenery, and its strength and challenges,

When most of us saw the river, it seemed like just a river. Experienced kayakers, however, immerses themselves in its full story, the different scales of rapids, positives and negatives, and the natural laws of the river. For them, nothing is to be feared, because it is understood, as they have learned as much as they can about it. Like rafters along the river, all of us need skills to navigate the constant challenges and changes that life presents and the different emotions we experience as a result. Life can be likened to a river with class-one to class-six scale rapids and some calm waters. We need the skills of a kayaker, yet we grow up with not enough education on how to navigate the rapids. With learning and critical knowledge, rafters transform fear to adventure, and that is how we need to live our lives.

Human beings are like an iceberg. There is more to us than people around us may see or what we may be willing to embrace of ourselves. Most of us need to take a self-tour to understand why we do what we do, and check if we really are living our own lives or the labels presented to us by others. The labels may be partially correct—some are empowering and some dis-empowering.

Exploring Your Iceberg

> *An important part of that understanding is knowing who we are and what we can do ... Ultimately, we must synthesize our understandings for ourselves.*
>
> —Howard Gardner

© Hannu Viitanen | Dreamstime.com

Exploring your iceberg helps to deepen your self-knowledge to understand who you really are and why you do the things you do. Most of us think we are the labels that others have said we are, and we rarely take time intentionally to understand what drives our behavior on a daily basis and then synthesize the knowledge.

We normally judge others based on what we see them do, but the visible part, the tip of the iceberg is on average about 9 percent of the whole story. Behavior is what we see in others or what others see of us and that is 9 percent of the whole story. However, influence to behave in a certain way comes from what lies underneath—the 91 percent that is invisible. How often do we see people doing something or behaving in a certain way, and we judge them? And are we correct? What lies beneath the surface is the invisible force that drives behavior, and emotions are part of that sphere of influence. Our **values, self-image, traits and motives** are part of what lies underneath, the invisible forces that drives our behavior. These define or shape our self-concept, which is what we think about ourselves Our self-concept influences our level of self-esteem, which is how we feel about ourselves. These under-the-surface forces trigger our emotions in any given situation. Diving deeper to explore what lies beneath in ourselves and in others will help us understand why people do what they do, or why we do what we do, bearing in mind that our action or inaction is dependent on how we feel.

Values

Part of what lies underneath the surface is your values. Your values give you an indication of what is important to you. Values influence our evaluation and interpretation of any given situation. That interpretation triggers a certain emotion, thereby governing the way we behave. Values develop from our life experiences, especially the early childhood experiences. For example, one of my values is independence; it is important to me. I don't want to be dominated, and this is based on my life experiences while growing up. Independence, for me, provides a form of certainty that is a human need. The more I feel independent, the more

I feel significant. The more the home environment presented some form of domination, expressed through abuse, the more I wanted to break free as I grew older. However, values are different for individuals, based on their experience and interpretation of the events that they encountered on their way. Two people can experience the same event and interpret and evaluate it differently; hence, two people can have different stories of the same event and develop different values and beliefs. On the other hand, for someone who grew up in a solid family, with love, laughter, and happiness, dependence or family unity may become a key value. Dependence for that person provides security and certainty.

I do believe that we all have a core value, and from the core value stems all our other values in the key areas of our lives, such as financial values, family values, vocational values, mental values, physical or health values, spiritual values, and social values. Values provide opportunities or threats in our lives. Our core value helps us to set the boundaries in the way we behave and connect with others—that is; if we are aware. Otherwise it becomes a source of frustration. When I am in an environment that support my values, I feel secure; for example, if the environment support independence, I am content and feel in control; hence, that is an opportunity for me to express myself better. But if the environment creates some form of dependence, I feel insecure, fearful, and uncertain. For example, I value financial freedom, and this stems from my core value of independence. So each time I find myself in a situation where I must borrow money, whether from the bank or from someone, my value is challenged. As a result, it is a threat, and I stress about it.

Our values sort of form rules of engagement—how we relate with others—forming and bonding in relationships or destroying relationships. I will trust someone who gives me independence; this creates harmony in the relationship. Each time this value is challenged, I feel disgusted, which creates tension. Understanding and knowing my values is important, but also knowing and understanding that everyone's values are different will assist me in relating better. Everyone is looking for an opportunity and not a threat, but often, because most of us are caught up in our own value and belief systems or what is important to us, we project this on to others. We want them to see what is important to us and for it to be equally as important to them, and this triggers conflict or disharmony. This is because we all have what is important to us, and it takes an acute awareness to honor other people's values.

Alignment of values becomes critical when we relate. How do I live out my values without threatening others, or how do I ensure that I am not threatened when others live out their values? In other words, how do I maximize my opportunities to reduce others' threats? If I relate to a person whose value is dependence or being dependable, how can I become independent in a dependent way? It sounds complicated, doesn't it?

Alignment of individual values also becomes very critical, as sometimes people have conflicting values, and this can create living in a confused state or being unaware what you are trying to portray as an individual. For example, you may value a certain lifestyle, which may mean fancy and expensive clothes, a fancy car, a fancy place to live, and eating out in fancy places. This lifestyle requires financing, and if you don't have a financial cushion, you may find yourself financing this through debt. If your financial value is financial freedom, this might be compromised by the core value of lifestyle.

Your core value is the axle that makes your wheel of life go around and make it easier for you to recognize a rewarding environment or to create a rewarding or fulfilling environment.

> *How different our lives are when we really know what is deeply important to us, and, keeping that picture in mind, we manage ourselves each day to be and to know what really matters most.*
>
> —Stephen Covey

Value Wheel (alignment example)

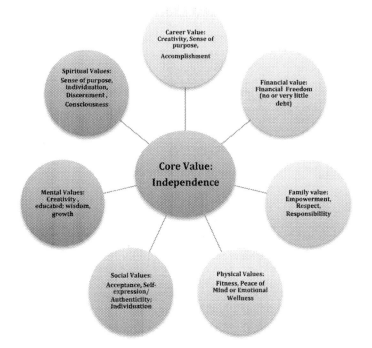

Exploration: Check Your Core Value

1. What is your core value? (check the list in appendix 1)
2. In each key area of your life (finances, family, spiritual, mental, career, social, and physical), pick at least two values
3. Does your core value influence your other values?

Self-image

Self-image is a mental picture of how we see ourselves or who we are. While we continue to grow, we may have an ideal self and a real self. Self-image is shaped by our formal and informal education system and by our peers as well. It can either be positive or negative, based on what we learned from the environment that shaped us. It can either be distorted or enhanced, and this consists of characteristics such as beautiful, ugly, talented, intelligent, stupid, kind, generous, selfish, lazy, hardworking, significant, insignificant, mean, or not good enough.

Your self-image will determine the value you place on yourself; your self-worth affects your self-esteem. If your self-esteem is positive, it means the shaping environment was enhancing, or that despite the negative environment, your inner power did not give power to the external force. I remember one time when my English teacher told me that I would get a D grade in English, because my English was terrible. I actually motivated myself to prove her wrong. I started reading more English novels to improve my English and got an A grade. Not everyone, though, is able to counter external influences and forces. If you struggle with confidence and low self-esteem, you may need to trace it back to its source, which could be an event, a person, or a word.

Our self-image also affects our self-talk—what we say to ourselves when no one else is listening. I don't mean the affirmations that are a way of trying to counter the voice inside you. While affirmations are good, it is also important to acknowledge the source of the problem and then try to fix it, rather than trying to wash a pot when you cannot see where the dirt is. Your self-image affects your behavior in the key areas of your life—financial, mental, career, spiritual, family, social, and physical. Sometimes people with low self-esteem or poor self-image cover up who they are by being arrogant, harsh, defensive, or angry. The great thing is that self-image is not fixed or static; it is ever-changing. Any positive self-image can get better, and a negative self-image can be transformed to make positive changes. Your self-image affects your dominant emotions.

Exploration: Self-image

1. Do you have a positive or negative self-image?
2. Pick three words that describe your self-image in these areas: home, work, finances, friends, family, physical, and mental (pick from a list of values in the appendix)
3. Is your self-image congruent with your ideal self?
4. How do these concepts of self affect your esteem and confidence?
5. Is there anything you do to cover up where there is negativity?
6. What are your dominant emotions as a result of self-image?

Traits

Traits are what make you stand out as an individual. Your traits are linked to your personality. Your positive traits influence self-appreciation, and negative traits influence self-criticism. Awareness of these will assist you in managing them to achieve the results you want. Traits also can be looked at as your strengths and weakness. Your weaknesses can be viewed as your overdone strengths, so all you need is to do is control the "volume" or the magnitude of expressing them. If you do not "control the volume," negative traits can stand in your way of achieving the desired results or goals. Knowing and understanding your personality will assist you in managing yourself as you become more aware of your behavior when things go well or when conflict arises. It also becomes easier to self-witness or just observe yourself.

Exploration: Traits

1. Pick your four positive attributes or traits.
2. Pick three negative traits.
3. Take a personality test—the Strength Deployment Inventory request on www.eMotions4Success.com

Motives

Your motives are the reasons why you do what you do, positive or negative. Self –help author, life coach and motivational speaker, Anthony Robbins identified six human needs that are motivators for behavior. These include love and connection, significance, certainty/comfort, variety/uncertainty, contribution, and growth. We all want to feel loved and love, and that gives us a sense of connection. This emotion can drive us to act in a certain way in pursuit of connection. Every human desires a sense of significance or feeling important; we want to matter and be accepted. With comfort comes certainty and ability to be in control. We all want to have the peace of mind that comes from certainty. On the other hand, while we want comfort, we also want variety that creates uncertainty. Growth is an essential element of every human being—this can be mental growth, financial growth, spiritual growth, career growth, and so on. We often do what we have to do in order to grow.

We all feel good when we contribute to humanity or to our loved ones, and we behave in a certain way to achieve that. Our motives are built upon our primal desires and very much linked to what we then value. Clarifying our motivation for doing what we do is crucial, so that we don't find ourselves with conflicting behaviors, and we can make better choices.

Your experience and how you respond to it in the first years of your life forms your values, self-image, and traits, and influences your motives. Your early life experiences create what you perceive as missing—your unmet needs—based on your individual interpretation and evaluation of events that occurred. Your unmet needs will inform what you pursue or will be the major driver of your behavior.

Exploration: Motives

1. What do you spend most of your energy on or most of your time doing?
2. What is your motive for doing what you do most of the time?

Develop Emotional Literacy

Nothing in life is to be feared. It is only to be understood.
—Marie Curie

A critical step in developing self-knowledge is enhancing emotional literacy. Most of us have never been educated about emotions in our formal and informal education system. The best I was ever taught about emotions as I was growing up was, "Think with your head, not your heart." What does this mean? Can a heart think? There is actually no common understanding on this, even though almost all of us have had this teaching. The other maxim, which also is taught, is "Don't be emotional about it." Again, what does this mean? Is there anyone who is not emotional? Are we describing what the person decides to do with the emotion, which is the action or behavior, rather than the emotion itself? Emotions are universal; we all have them. However, we use them differently— some deny them or suppress them; some overindulge and let their emotions run out of control. Most people are afraid of their own emotions. They would rather not acknowledge them, or they try to escape from them, which is a futile exercise. We are all born with emotions as a primal survival tool.

In developing self-knowledge, we need to be aware of our tendencies. Emotions influence what we do or don't do. As previously mentioned emotions are the second biggest killer after medicine, but in as much as emotions can be dangerous, we don't need to fear them, suppress, or deny them; we need to understand them. Emotions show life so there are powerful and useful we just

11

need to understand them. When we understand them, we can use them effectively to make optimum decisions. When I start a session on emotional literacy in my Emotional Intelligence sessions, I usually ask people, "What is literacy?" or "How do you know you are literate?" The response is usually that they can read and write. And the follow-up question is, "What is emotional literacy?" And we sort of get stuck! I ask participants to list ten emotions, but rarely is anyone able to list ten. Most people describe their actions or their state of being as emotions. Emotions drive our actions and inactions on a daily basis, yet most of us never really pay attention to what we are feeling, let alone know what we are feeling.

Exploration: Emotional Literacy

1. List ten emotions.
2. Are you feeling something right now?
3. What are you feeling?
4. How do you know you are feeling. or where do you find it?

Just check how long it took you to list ten emotions and how many you listed are actually emotions. Did you notice that you were baffled by trying to connect with your own emotions? If you struggled, you are alone! We have never been educated, formally or informally, about emotions.

Emotional literacy is the ability to accurately identify emotions, recognize their source, and understand and appropriately communicate the emotion or express the emotion. Emotions are electro-chemical signals, released from the brain, to affect every living cell in our bodies. According to research done by 6seconds. org, that process of releasing the electro-chemical signal takes about six seconds. Each emotion has a lifespan between 90 and 120 seconds. What that means is that each time you continue to feel something after 120 seconds, it is a choice. And choice can be intentional or unintentional—either way, you are making a choice.

What this means is that you send the same signal to the brain to release the same electro-chemical signal. The event has passed, but you are reliving the event by telling yourself a story about what happened and then interpreting, evaluating, and reevaluating it.

The subconscious brain does not know the difference between what it sees in its environment, what it remembers or imagines, it will release electro-chemical signals that match the information you gave it. Have you ever thought about something that happened in the past and were happy or sad or angry? The emotional brain does not know it is in the past or future until you rationalize it. That is, your conscious brain kicks in to indicate that it is past or future; hence, there is no need to worry about it now, but just it accept that it happened and learn from it.

The Latin word *emovere* means to move through and out, which is the same word for the English word *emotion*. So literally, emotions are supposed to move through and out. You are supposed to release the emotions, allowing them to flow continuously in and out, like the waves of the river. If you hold on to them, you stagnate and become toxic if they are negative. Allow them to flow continuously.

In understanding emotions, it is critical to build and enhance emotional literacy—the ability to identify the emotion and how the emotion expresses itself in our bodies. Emotional literacy and navigating emotions is a continuous journey, not a destination. It is a journey to transformation. We cannot manage what we do not know. Emotional literacy is the foundation of self-awareness, of knowing yourself. Emotions have different intensities, from low energy to high energy, and they are either positively charged or negatively charged. Emotions are neither good nor bad; they are feedback loops, telling us how things are within us and around us. We are responsible for how we feel. Events may happen or others may do or say something to us, but it is our evaluation and interpretation of what has happened that will make us feel whatever we feel.

In building emotional literacy, we need to understand the different energy levels of emotions. An example of the different energy levels of emotions would be moving from annoyance to anger to rage. So these are the different energy levels of anger, or scales of rapids. The higher the energy level of an emotion, the more it becomes a derailer, or makes us unable to perform in a positive way, as it takes energy away from us or gives us temporary energy for destruction. If negatively charged, it is more life-threatening, just like the class five of rapids. The waves are high, and we feel that we are overwhelmed; hence, no longer in control. The forces of the emotion mostly pull us away from the positive outcomes we want. And this is where we need the skills of a kayaker to paddle backward and then hard forward to move forward. When navigating emotions, we also need to understand that we are dealing with an invisible force that drives behavior and performance.

In a state of a high-energy negative emotion, we also experience diminishing focus—that is, we are no longer concerned about the outcomes we want or concerned about the impact of our actions or inactions on others. We want to get rid of the problem, but the manner in which it is done might create other problems. The emotional brain is the survival center, so each time there is something that the emotional brain perceives as life-threatening, our defense bars go up. When we feel angry, the first instinct is to want to attack to defend ourselves, but this might not get us the results we want. Experiencing the emotion and allowing it flow through becomes critical instead of reacting automatically as though there is no space between what happened, how you feel and what you decide to do about it. Acknowledging how you are feeling and questioning the emotion will help you to get insight so you can choose a response or behavior that gets you what you want.

The diagram below illustrates more. Emotions start with low intensity and then build up. In the middle layer are basic emotions. The emotions in the inner circle, whether positively charged or negatively charged, are derailers. Each time you experience derailers, you cannot perform, or you are stuck with the results you don't want.

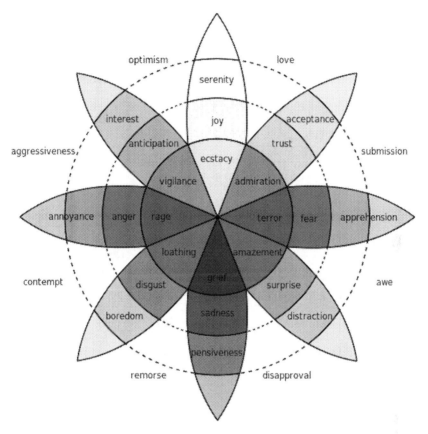

Reprinted by permission of American Scientist magazine of Sigma Xi, the Scientific Research Society.

These emotions show what we may be experiencing in our internal world. Most of us tend to describe ourselves by how we feel; for example, we say, *I am angry*, and that energizes the emotion in our bodies. Emotions are temporary. They are in constant flow, coming and going. Hence, we cannot use permanent statements like *I am angry*; we need to acknowledge that it is an emotion by saying, *I am feeling angry*. This becomes the first step in managing or navigating the emotion. This helps us to choose our response to not react, as most of us are caught up in a reaction rut—*I am angry*; therefore, I attack. Flee, fight, or freeze instincts kick in, and we start operating in our survival mode, even though the event happening is not life-threatening. When negatively charged, we experience a diminishing focus—our behavior takes us away from the results we want. With a diminishing focus, we forget that we have a choice, and we can exercise that choice by being "response-able"—that is, responding to the best of our ability. We can focus on the outcomes and choose a behavior that gets us what we want, instead of being remotely controlled by our emotions or being emotionally hijacked.

In managing emotions, it important to note on the map that emotions intensify to the center—that is, they are highly energized at the center, and it is easier to transform a low-energy emotion than a high-energy emotion. It is easier to move from one neighbor to the next and to move from the one thing to its opposite; for example, from boredom to acceptance. Transforming of emotions can be done by questioning the emotion. Here, what matters is the quality of questioning or simply releasing the negative emotion. Hoarded negative emotions can trip you backward when you want to move forward, as they are now stored in your subconscious mind. While wanting to move forward, you react to what *has happened*, not what *is happening*. Tracing these past negative emotions and transforming or releasing them becomes vital to moving forward.

Notably, the emotional map shows that there are more negative emotions than positive. It is easier; therefore, to have your life dominated by negative or unpleasant feelings. It takes a conscious effort to remain in the positive zone that enhances your flow state. The quality of your emotions influences the quality of your life. Research shows that most workplaces are dominated by fear and anxiety. Most people work for the better part of their lives, the better part of the week, and the better part of the day. Also, because emotions intensify in energy as you keep telling yourself a story about what has happened, it is easy to hoard emotions from the past or even from your childhood. If you do not manage these emotions, they will affect your well-being and success.

Individuals normally engage in self-destructive behaviors or in behaviors that do not respect the dignity of others when trying to give themselves relief from these unpleasant and uncomfortable emotions. Such behaviors may include alcoholism, a flashy lifestyle, compulsive sexual behavior, hot anger, crime, and so on. To trace the emotions that influence these behaviors, they have to be conversant with their life stories; they must be willing to know how they got to this place in their lives.

Questioning basic emotions

Quality questions create a quality life. Successful people ask better questions, and as a result, they get better answers.
—Anthony Robbins

When you question your emotions, you gain understanding of yourself. What are your dominant emotions? How have they contributed to the way things are in your life—financially, socially at work or at home, mentally, physically, and spiritually? Do you experience empowering or disempowering emotions? Are they future-related, past-related or present-related emotions?

You can learn to manage your emotions. Where you are today in life, in all the key areas of life, is a result of what you have done or not done—actions or inactions. Actions and inactions are driven by how you feel. Every decision you make every day is influenced by how you feel, even the decision to wake up each morning. This means you need to constantly navigate emotions to achieve the results you want. One way of managing emotions is to ask yourself questions that propel you forward, rather than get you stuck.

Look at the emotional map. The emotions in the center ring of the emotional wheel are the eight basic emotions from which all other emotions emanate, differing in energy levels. To manage an emotion, you need to correctly identify it and its source and then question it to manage it, remembering that it is neither good nor bad and that emotions are information. They are basic messages from you to you. Some people experience displacement—that is, they had a stressful day at work, so they take it out on their children or spouse. Or they may have a delayed response—they had a conversation with someone and during that time, they froze and were unable to speak their mind. Then, two or more days later, they still are having a discussion with themselves, thinking, *I should have said* … In most cases, that does not create the opportunity to say what they want to say. Displacement and delayed responses are indications of how emotions can override our rational brain.

Anger

> *No one else "makes us angry." We make ourselves angry when we surrender control of our attitude.*
>
> —Jim Rohn

What is blocking your way? Where do you want to go? What options do you have? Feeling angry is natural and human; everyone feels angry sometimes. Anger is a protective mechanism. However, in trying to protect yourself, you may engage in destructive behaviors that harm you or others. And because anger is a negatively charged electro-chemical signal, you will release toxic substances into your bloodstream; hence, you need to shorten the lifespan of anger in your body. The right questions can assist you in releasing anger faster, as you engage in positive behavior to solve your challenges. Anger can be used to fuel you to take action or develop courage and interest to understand your challenges. It can also assist you to create solutions or accept what you cannot change. Bottled-up anger, on the other hand, can make you bitter or aggressive; anger from a previous event that has not been released can energize current anger to rage.

When you feel angry, someone or something is blocking your way. Identifying that obstacle is important to solving the problem. Remember that you experience a diminishing focus when you are negatively charged. It is important to remind yourself of the results you want so that you don't engage in a behavior that takes you away from those results, which is what normally happens when you feel angry. When the results you want are clear in your head, it helps to focus on the outcomes you want, not on the problem or obstacle. In options thinking, you are now choosing a behavior that gets you what you want. Instead of reacting, you are responding. It is important to note that anger is always a secondary emotion; you feel something first before you feel angry. It is always easier to transform the primary emotion than the secondary emotion.

Exploration: Transforming Anger

In a training session of transforming anger, one lady indicated that she felt angry when her husband did not clean the pool when she asked. Her husband's reaction might have been refusal or giving reasons for not doing it, but the lady's response here is more important—she must decide what she wants to focus on: the problem or the solution. In this case, her husband was the obstacle because, according to her, he had refused to clean the pool for the past couple of months. Her initial feelings might be disapproval, annoyance, or even anger. I asked her what she wanted, and her response was, "I want the pool cleaned." The follow-up was asking her what options she had. We explored her options: clean it herself, hire someone to clean it, communicate differently in her husband's value system (which might be the language he understands), or accept that he will not clean the pool. This way, her anger would be transformed into a positive emotion—happy that the pool is cleaned, happy that there is a solution to her challenge, or accepting that this is the way things are.

Explore your own anger and see what is it that makes you feel angry and how you can transform it. Anger can be useful or destructive, empowering or disempowering, depending on how you decide to use it. It can fuel you to initiate change or to become despondent. Sometimes, people are angry about a past experience, and they project it into the present.

Anticipation

What important thing is coming? What is the impact? Is this really what you want? Are you prepared?

In most cases, anticipation creates other emotions, like anxiety or excitement or sadness, depending on whether what you are looking forward to is positive or negative. When you anticipate, you bring a future event or condition into the present moment, causing you to look forward to pleasure or pain. Anticipation is a powerful, persuasive emotion that can trigger changing of the mind. If you anticipate pain, you may move away from the event, and if you anticipate pleasure, you move toward it. Anticipation also can create disappointment or relief, if what you are expecting to happen doesn't happen.

Anticipation is the source of all creativity and innovation by imagining things that are not there or something that hasn't happened yet. Positive anticipation does not need to be transformed; it just needs to be balanced or intentional—this will avoid negativity when what we are looking forward to does not happen. Most people anticipate negative things or anticipate positive things without a matching action to create the desired state. Hence, the end result is still negative—disappointment. Creating pleasurable anticipation is the source for hope that can take us through and out of challenging times. Anticipation also assists us in setting goals; for example, what are you looking forward to? To become what? To have what? And what do you need to do to get that result? What we are living today is something we anticipated and took action to achieve it. Intentional anticipation creates enthusiasm for action.

The example I use regularly is that of anticipating marriage. The way most of us are socialized, the clock seems to tick for women, such that at a certain stage, some women feel pressured to get married. They look forward to marriage, but most do not ask, *is this really what I want*? That is, they do not evaluate the candidate before them or define their primary objective for marriage. What follows, then, is marriage for the wrong reasons, which may end up in divorce, death, or destruction.

Where anticipation is intentional, it helps to align your goals to others, where other people are involved.

Exploration: Intentional Anticipation

1. What do you look forward to every day?
2. Why do you look forward to it, or what do you want to achieve in any given situation?
3. What preparation or action are you taking to see it come to pass?

Joy

What good or positive thing is going on? How do you maintain it?

Joy is our default state of being. We are born happy, and we learn to be sad. Think about how happy children are most of the time when they fully express themselves. As we grow older, joy becomes a mere visitor. For some, it visits once a year, like Christmas; for others, once a month, when it's payday. When was the last time you experienced joy? This emotion does not need to be transformed but maintained. Most people reserve joy for specific events or conditions. To undo the sadness you have learned over the years, you have to make a conscious choice to be happy and find ways to return to that default state of being. Identifying some of the things that steal your joy is important. These may include fear and worry of the future, your belief on how things should be, comparing your life with others, loss of loved ones, negative self-talk, and ungratefulness. Heightened awareness will help you be in touch with the joy-stealers and release them.

In a marriage, most people enjoy the honeymoon period but a few months later, they don't enjoy or appreciate each other. Or you might get a new job, and you are so excited about this new opportunity for the first few weeks. Soon, though, you start complaining or become bored with the job. As much as we love certainty, we love variety to avoid monotony, so you can maintain joy by looking at various ways of living out what is important to you.

Exploration: Maintaining Joy

1. What makes you happy?
2. How often do you do it?
3. What are various ways you can do this?
4. What are you thankful for? Find three things to be thankful for every day, even in anything you currently perceive as negative.

Trust

> *You may be deceived if you trust too much, but you will live in torment if you do not trust enough.*
> -Dr. Frank Crane

What do you want to connect with? Why is this important to you? We live in a very volatile world, where trust is becoming more and more difficult, yet we cannot live without trust. Each time we do not trust, negative emotions, like suspicion, disgust, fear, or anger, creep in. Trust is linked to our values and beliefs. When you trust, you embrace or accept someone, because that person connects to your values and beliefs. Your beliefs can change, and your values can be aligned to other people's values to enable trust. Trust can be influenced positively or negatively by a previous event or experience.

Here, it is easy to punish others for something they have no clue about. Due to a past experience, you may find it hard to trust, or you punish yourself for other people's behaviors, and you feel angry for being betrayed. That anger is self-punishment, as it does not serve you. Remember that negative emotions restrict flow in every area of your life. You trust what connects to your values, and each time someone crosses your values, it becomes difficult to trust. However, your values are for you to live out, not for others, as every individual has his or her own values. When you accept others for their values and try to align your values to theirs, if it is necessary, you can trust them. Trust is the glue that binds relationships together, whether in the corporate world or in your personal life. Trust influences behaviors and performances.

Exploration: Building Trust

1. Think about a person you trust. Why do you trust him or her?
2. Is it linked to your values?
3. How can you align your values to others' values?
4. Think about a person you do not trust. Why do you not trust him or her?
5. Try to think what could be important to that person. What are his or her values?
6. Are that person's values different from yours?
7. Can you accept that person for his or her values without trying to make the person share your values?

8. In what ways can you align your different values?
9. Is there any past experience that affects your trust for others or even for yourself now?
10. If there is a past issue or experience, choose a tool or technique to release, dissolve, or bring it to acceptance—tools like the emotional freedom techniques.

Fear

What is in jeopardy? Is it really in jeopardy?

Most of your fears exist only in your head. It is the stories you tell yourself about what could happen. The emotion of fear keeps your survival alarm bell on alert—the fight, flight, or freeze syndrome. As the alarm bell is alerted, it continually tries to search and pick out from your environment what it evaluates as possible danger, and it goes off. You are likely to be triggered every day by issues or events that are not real dangers but that are perceived as dangers by the amygdala—a part of the emotional brain. For example, your boss screams at you, or your spouse or boyfriend/girlfriend does not pick up the phone when you call. When you are triggered, you then release the stress hormones cortisol and adrenaline, which either make you fight, become defensive, freeze, or avoid or run away from the issue or event. Many people miss out on opportunities to be loved, to create wealth, or to become more fulfilled as a result of fear. It paralyzes them from taking action, or their behavior, in an effort to protect themselves, takes them away from the results they want.

Fear can also be triggered by a past event. Most fears are linked to the common fears, which include fear of death, fear of failure, fear of the unknown (known), survival fears, fear of change, and fear of pain or being hurt. The fear of pain or being hurt can manifest as fear of rejection. We are born with two basic fears: fear of falling or heights and fear of loud noises. Have you ever thrown a child in the air? What does he do? He will only start giggling after being tossed up a couple of times, because then he knows he is safe. Have you ever screamed near a baby? You will get the same reaction you got when you threw the baby in the air for the first time. All the other fears we have are learned. Just as we have our fears or have been taught our fears, we can unlearn them by confronting them in a safe way. You may say to yourself, *my fear of spiders is not a big deal,* but each time you think or imagine spiders, it disturbs your flow by disrupting your energy flow. All your fears go everywhere with you—they can affect every area of your life. I had a fear of water because I nearly drowned when I was younger while swimming in the river. Still, I decided to go river rafting. It was safe; I had a life jacket and experts around me.

Fear has the power to kill in an instant, like a bullet, or keep you in a state of anxiousness. Being anxious all the time can make you paranoiac, and this is a slow killer. A family member said to me, after her mother passed away, that she did not know how she would live, as her pillar had been taken away. She was so afraid, and a few months later, she was diagnosed with cancer. In less than two years after her mother passed, this woman also died. Fear may not have caused her cancer, but it is possible that it fueled it to spread quickly.

Exploration: Confronting Your Fears in a Safe Way

1. What are you afraid of?
2. Is it real danger or just a story you are telling yourself?
3. Are you willing to let go of the fear?
4. How could you increase safety from the possibility of the manifestation of that fear?
5. Try tapping the fear using the emotional freedom technique.

Surprise

What is happening without warning? Is it pleasant or unpleasant?

The emotion of surprise is linked to an unexpected change, and it is reactive. Whether pleasant or unpleasant, it can lead to shock. Where it does not lead to shock, it is followed immediately by another emotion, which could be joy, fear or sadness, or anger. Surprise occurs as a result of the gap between our expectations or assumptions and reality. This also opens a window to learning, as it exposes us to our ignorance. My husband and family recently organized a surprise birthday party for me. I was not expecting it at all; in my mind, I had pictured a day spent alone, writing, as my husband works away, and my son had gone off to a friend's for the weekend. I even planned to have my hair done, and as I was about to step out of the house, there was everyone downstairs. I was surprised and even had a mini-shock, as I was not expecting it. I was happy the whole day, because it was a pleasant surprise. Events that can surprise include an employee resigning without warning, spouse or boyfriend/girlfriend leaving, loss of a loved one, and so on. Whenever unexpected change happens, the challenge is in how you respond to it. While you may drive change, you cannot drive all change; hence, there is need to anticipate some change over which you may have no control and anticipate ways to bring the changes to acceptance when they happen. Surprise can lead to denial when the issue or event is not accepted, and denial breeds negative emotions.

Exploration: Managing Unexpected Change

1. What unexpected events have occurred in your life?
2. How did you handle them?
3. Could you have handled them differently?
4. What unexpected change could happen that you have no control over?

5. What responses could help you to bring the change to acceptance?

Sadness

What do you love or are pleased with that you will cease to have? Can it be replaced? Can you live without it? Emotions of sadness emanate from a sense of loss or being disadvantaged, which result from some attachment you develop from ownership. When it is yours, you want to hold on to it with all that is within you. The truth, though, is that you can live without anything that you call your own. At some point, you have lived without it or will live without it, and life will carry on. While it is normal and acceptable to be sad and not deny that feeling, what matters is how much time you spend on being sad. The longer the time you spend being sad, the longer the disruption to your flow.

As sadness is nurtured, it can intensify to grief, depression, or semi-permanent anger. Have you ever come across people who are just angry or who look for any opportunity to get angry? You need to transform sadness into a positive emotion before it stops you from living, even though you are alive. The way to transform sadness is to acknowledge the event or to accept it, not to deny it or try to delete it. When people want to maintain the feeling of sadness, whether consciously or unconsciously, they will offer explanations such as, "If only I had …"; or "If only someone had … if only this was not done …"; or "If only this did not happen …" or "I should have …"; or "Someone should have …" They tell themselves or others a story that could have happened, which did not happen, avoiding looking at what has happened, which is the reality.

Like surprise, there is a gap between what we expect to happen and what is happening. Like losing a loved one, you may wish the loved one had lived longer, or that you'd said good-bye, or that you'd had time to tell your loved one how you feel. We cannot reverse or recover things we have no control over, and we may have to accept other people's behaviors to transform the emotion into positive energy.

Exploration: Accepting Loss

1. Is there an issue or event that makes you feel sad?
2. What is the story you tell yourself about the event?
3. Are there shoulds, ifs, and musts in your story?
4. What control did you (or do you) have over it?
5. Can you recover or reverse the situation?
6. Is it possible you are punishing yourself for someone else's behavior or for the irreversible laws of nature?
7. Are you being too hard on yourself? (Practice self-empathy—you did the best you could with the resources and knowledge you had at that time.)
8. Practice gratitude. What three things can you be thankful for about the event. (In the case of death, how can you celebrate the life lived. instead concentrating only on the loss?)

Disgust

What value/values has/have been infringed or violated? Why is this important to you?

When your values are infringed or violated, it is easy to feel disgusted. Disgust is an emotion that evokes withdrawing from an unclean or potentially harmful physical issue or substance, like vomit, or person who behaves out of line with your values. There is a tendency to liken people's behaviors with unclean objects or features, such as he/she is rotten, he/she is dead to me, he/she is an "a–hole." This shows feelings of disgust due to violated values. Most people can be triggered or disgusted by someone else's behavior without realizing their reaction is a reflection about them—what is important to them, not what is important to the other person. Unaware, we just react without knowing the value ourselves so that we can make it known to others. In transforming disgust, follow a four-step approach:

Step one: Each time you feel disgusted, *uncover* the value that has been violated.

Step two: *Rethink* the value. For example, while I may value independence, do I have to define independence by not being told what to do? At work, it may not be possible, because I have a boss whose duty is to see that I perform and give me instructions, even though I value independence. Another way to look at it is this: how is what I am doing now enabling me to be independent in other areas to ultimately become who I want to be?

Step three: *Communicate* the value and find ways to *align* it to other people's values. Most of us have values that guide us but consciously unaware of them, hence unable to communicate them to others.

Step four: *Adjust* the value. Even though I value independence, I can get more and work better in a team with multiple ideas. Also, it is essential to understand that this is not a shared value; hence, while I live it out, I should not expect others to live it out, as it may not be their value. Where this value creates a challenge with important goals or outcomes to achieved, I can borrow a behavior to achieve the desired outcome, so I will not be changing the value but creating multiple behavioral options to obtain the results I want. So the value is not necessarily being changed; I am just changing a behavior for a short while, bearing in mind that my values inform my beliefs and behaviors. Disgust is not always about other people. It is possible to have self-disgust. Some people do not like who they are, how they look, or what they have done in the past—they have broken their own values.

Exploration: Transforming Disgust

1. Is there an issue, event, or person that makes you feel disgusted?
2. What value of yours do/did they violate?
3. What action or behavior do you currently see as coherent with that value?
4. Is it possible that that value can still be fulfilled by behaving differently?
5. With reference to 1, above, did you communicate your value?
6. How can you adjust or align the value(s) with other people's value(s) without a feeling of disgust or loss?

Become the Hero of Your Story

> *Until you make the unconscious conscious, it will direct your life and you will call it fate.*
>
> —C. G. Jung

The body remembers everything that has happened to it. Our emotions help us to store up information in our unconscious minds. The unconscious mind weaves a story of our lives. Most people are minors of their stories, because they minimize or belittle themselves by denying or not acknowledging the story that shaped who they are. It is difficult to be authentic and confident without accepting your story. Most of our childhood experiences are lying in the subconscious mind, and they influence our adult behavior from under the radar. Most programming or conditioning happens before we reach nine years of age. We are what we learned, but not necessarily all we learned actually serves us. The good news is that we can unlearn it and learn new ways of being to become who we want to be. As a result of learning from socialization, it is possible to go through life, living someone else's life. What do I mean by that?

After going through a client's story with her, we both realized that it took almost thirty years of her life to discover that she was living her mother's life and somehow, also her father's life. Her father was abusive, physically and emotionally. She and her siblings grew up witnessing physical and verbal abuse; obviously, that translates to emotional abuse. In her adult age, her story became that *she does not want to be dominated or abused*, and she disliked her father for the abuse. That story shaped who she became in relationships. Anywhere she sensed domination or what she perceived as abuse, she fought it and would quickly move on. She would fight at school, work, and with her family members, as long as she perceived abuse or domination, subconsciously re-creating her mother and father's story. She inherited certain beliefs from the environment in which she grew up about relationships and how to relate. What is also important to note here is that in her adult life, she reacted to what had happened, not to what was happening, thereby making decisions influenced by emotions of a past event, not what had been or was happening in the moment.

You may have inherited certain beliefs, attitudes, behaviors, and perceptions from the environment that shaped you. That includes the school system, your parents or guardians, the church, and the home environment.

I like what author of Emotional Maturity, Duane Youngblood says about home: "*Home really matters and if you are upset with culture today, you will not fix it by going after children. Home must be addressed because it is the cell that all society is built upon. If home is a mess, society will be a mess too. If home is filled with pain, society will be too. We must deal with home, and the more we bring voice to the issues we gather at home, the more we will see emotional maturity in our lives.*"

The challenge with a home background is that some stories are never told. You form your own perception and beliefs, based on what you see happening, and you never understand why it is happening. Certain information that may be useful on your journey is not available, as not many people can tell their stories.

Another client of mine related a story about seeing her stepbrother from her mother's side at her mother's funeral for the first time, and he was a replica of their mother. No one had ever mentioned that there was a stepbrother. It had remained a secret. Imagine the surprise and the shock. She said she could not help staring at him and asking herself why they never had talked about him.

Maya Angelou said, "*There is no greater agony than bearing an untold story inside you.*" My question is, how did the parents feel all of their lives about not talking about the story? Our stories connect us to our destiny and our stories are part of the bigger picture connecting one person to the other. Stories connect us to our feelings and telling them help us to navigate the emotions. Any untold story distorts the destiny of many and as a result of an untold story, how many other stories were untold or will not be told? How many and what lessons are lost?

Who are you without your conditioning? What stories—told, untold, and the ones you created—have shaped the person you have become? What experiences or events have shaped who you are today? When we see things happening, we give them meaning by evaluating and interpreting them so that we can understand them—that is creating a story. If others give us their meaning of what is happening and we accept their meaning, then we take their meaning of the event. Any meaning we end up with shapes our experience, unless we change the meaning. The meaning we give forms the basis of our belief system, and this belief system is formed early in life. Unless we change it, we keep on evaluating and interpreting new events and experiences to validate our prior conclusions, meanings, and beliefs. This filtering of information to support our existing beliefs happens unconsciously. This is why acute awareness is critical to witness that unconscious filtering and change it, if it is necessary to do so (and in most cases, it is).

Self-knowledge is a continuous journey of understanding and knowing your true essence—the journey you have walked thus far and understanding your authentic self. Knowing your strengths, weakness, beliefs, tendencies, boundaries, limits, and your purpose—that is your true voice. Some experiences we go through make us more vocal, defensive, blaming, or timid or silence us forever.

In developing self-awareness, you also need to know how you have navigated the rapids of life, up to where you are today, with the knowledge, strengths, and skill sets you have. How did you get to this place in your life, and where do you go from here? In leveraging the power of your story, what key emotional stamina or assets did you portray? What key values have you lived by, and what are the possible areas of improvement? Most of us react to what has happened, not to what is happening. We always go back to experience. The challenge is that most of us go back to experience unaware. We use what has happened to react to what is happening here and now. While experience is good, it can be misleading and lead to outcomes we do not want. Most of the time, conditions have changed from our past. From experience or from our history comes beliefs that direct us daily most of the time unaware.

Our upbringing has shaped who we are or what we have become. We are programmed or conditioned to think and behave the way we do. Every life has a set of challenges and a set of good events. Most of us, however, would rather forget a part of our story or try to delete it. Some of us think our lives are full of drama, so we never share it with anyone, not even ourselves. We hardly look at our whole experience, as far as we can remember it as a whole story. We normally pick certain chapters that we want to think about at one time. In building self-awareness, the goal is never to escape our stories but to make them sacred.

When we do this exercise in the Emotional Intelligence course, there is a lot of resistance and resentment. People do not want to tell their stories and if they do, many edit, forge, or copy or give an abstract of their stories. What I know now, though, is that your story of where you have been does not change. It changes going forward by acknowledging what happened in the past and navigating forward to create what you want and to become who you want to be. Where do I go from here? What do I want to create? Our past may be made up of things we created or things created by other people—for example, parents and guardians—and they too did the best they could with the knowledge they had. Nothing stops you, however, from questioning your past (instead of judging it) to change the course of your destiny. You need to understand your past.

> *We are all captives of a story.*
> —Daniel Quinn

We are emotional products of what our journeys have created. We have inherited some behaviors, beliefs and values. Our past experience affects our evaluation and interpretation of events in the present moment. And for us to be aware of the product that we are, as a result of systems that shaped us, we need to get in touch with our stories. How did I get to this place in my life? According to the societal standards, when we look at our environments, it is never appropriate for most of us to share the stories.

You may argue that it is not professional for me to share my life story with my work colleagues, because it is personal. Often, however, the personal affects the public. And when we share our stories, others around us can connect with us at a human level. We understand that this person has been angry, just like us; disappointed, just like us; has regrets, just like us; has emotions, just like us; has been confused, just like us; has experienced physical suffering and pain, just like us; wants to be loved, just like us; wants to be healthy, just like us; wants to be free, just like us; and wants to be accepted, just like us. Telling our stories as they are sets us free. Some of us think that running away or denying our stories is freedom. Telling our stories helps us to connect the dots of our lives, reconnect the pieces, and expand into our wider selves. We become the hero of our own stories.

In telling stories, others decide to focus only on the positive, sanitizing their stories, focusing only on the triumphs, as dictated by external standards. These people think they are doing themselves or others a favor, but all they are doing is shrinking inside and becoming a minor of their story, that is minimizing your role in your life. Most of us don't tell our stories often, because we are self-conscious. When we look at past events that we perceive as negative, we become sensitive. We cry for events that have actually built the hero in us. While crying is not a bad thing, our tears should be tears of joy and celebration, acknowledging our wider selves—the hero in us that managed to conquer the obstacles.

Telling our life stories, too, should be a ritual—the way we exit each year by adding another chapter. That chapter will be made up of the highs and lows of the key areas we all want to fulfill, which are our relationships, financial freedom, mental growth, career growth, spiritual freedom and growth, and physical health and well-being, as well as the changes we encountered and the insights from all the events. As we add another chapter, it is also an opportunity to press the refresh button of our lives, to update the previous chapters. Updating means with the new knowledge we acquired, we have to see past events differently. In hindsight, with what we know now, we can certainly improve going forward, thereby transforming our behavior and continuing to grow.

If we continue to see the events in our past the same way we did when they occurred, then there is no transformation. Even the Book of Life says in Romans 12:2, "And be not conformed to this world: but be ye transformed by the renewing of your mind, that ye may prove what [is] that good, and acceptable, and perfect, will of God." We have to update or refresh to see things differently, change our perspectives, and challenge our beliefs to become who we are meant to be or who we want to become.

When we refresh and update, we not only are creative, but we also recharge and free ourselves from a past burden. Our decision making going forward is sharpened and forges ahead toward our goals by responding instead of reacting. Anything we continue to see in the same way carries the same emotional baggage and weight it had when it happened; if it is negative, it does not serve us. Research shows that any unresolved emotion will find somewhere to settle in our body and show up as a form of ailment or disease.

Exploration: Reflection of Your Life

> *If we choose to conquer, we have to first choose to confront.*
> —author unknown

And remember that if you find any scars or wounds,

> *Our wounds are trophies, evidence that we have conquered something great"*
> - TD Jakes

And if you find any pain, the journey is not complete.

> *Your pain is the breaking of the shell that encloses your understanding*
> -Khalil Gibran

Reflection of your life refers to looking back and tracing the path you have walked to get to where you are today. It is a combination of all of your life's experiences, all the things you have done or not done, and all the choices you have made. It's a reflection on the highs and lows of your life—the experiences of your life that were good or devastating.

Take about twenty minutes on your own to do the following exercise: Draw a picture that reflects your life from as far back as you can remember into your childhood. If you do not have a creative talent, you can reflect your life story in five-year stages; for example, 5–10 years, 11–15 years. Your drawing or staged story may include the following:

1. The most significant, life-changing events that shaped or influenced the person you are, which affected the direction of your life, your successes, your moments of greatest joy, your challenges, and your moments of sadness
2. The influential people in your life—people you feel were most significant in shaping your belief system, your personality, and your life, both in a positive and negative way
3. The values you lived out or developed; dreams you pursued or abandoned; passions you developed and pursued; and goals you set and achieved or failed to achieve that impacted and guided you through your journey
4. The part yet unlived—your hopes; who you want to become
5. Whatever is holding you back
6. Whatever you are thankful for and what you regret
7. How all this helped you (regrets and things you are thankful for) to be become who you are today
8. Any unresolved issues and whether you would like to resolve them

The Web That Drives Your Life—Your Patterns

Patterns are where dreams go to die.

—author unknown

© Arjenschippers | Dreamstime.com

As we sailed down the river, I saw spiderwebs on the trees by the riverside. Some webs were deserted, and some had spiders still on them. Spiders make these webs for security reasons—that is, to catch their prey, as well as to live in the webs. It is also a transport network; spiders move faster in their webs than they move on the ground. But the webs also form beautiful patterns. Like spiders, you weave patterns. These patterns help you to create certainty in your life, which is one key human need. They also provide a form of security, because you are familiar with them. They help you to move quickly, instead of needing to stop to figure out things.

Yes, I'm still referring to self-knowledge and self-exploration. We are creatures of habit, so we do have habits that become patterns in our lives. We should not only be aware of them but should understand how and at which part of the journey they developed. While patterns are not totally bad, they do get outdated. They need to be renewed, and some of them should be totally abandoned, because they no longer serve us. Unlike spiders, however, not many of us are able to notice when a pattern is old and should be abandoned to create a new one. We must never stop weaving. And yes, some patterns are dream killers— the things you do or the behavior in which you engage that does not help achieve your dream. These patterns can be behavioral patterns, thought patterns, emotional patterns, financial patterns, spiritual patterns, or social and relating patterns. What is it that you do or think regularly that has given you the results you have today?

Patterns include the following: starting something but not finishing; spending money that you don't have; emotional shopping (you are upset, so the only way to heal is to use a temporary tranquilizer—shopping); defensive behavior; manipulative behavior; aggressive behavior; giving in all the time; not speaking out; being a victim; blaming; being upset about things you can not change every day; not asking for what you want; displacing your emotions; avoidance; obsessive behavior; perfectionist behavior; being a control freak—the list is endless.

Patterns can be as simple as traveling the same road to your workplace every day for five years. On the day that road closes, it's a mean mind drama as you try to teach your brain an alternative route. When you follow certain patterns, your brain becomes comfortable and cannot be creative and innovative. We all have patterns, and we need to constantly check if they need an upgrade so that we can perform better. Not all patterns are destructive. You may be a good listener, a time-conscious person, flexible, someone who considers alternatives, and a fact gatherer. Identifying these patterns is the essence of renewal to ensure that what you do can sustain your best initiatives, goals, and dreams, instead of creating self-sabotage. To change a pattern, you have to create another pattern, and that requires discipline.

Sometimes we make others pay for our patterns; for example, your pattern may be lack of trust as a result of an event that happened in your life, and this may make you treat everyone who comes your way with suspicion, punishing them for something about which they have no clue. Who is paying the price for your patterns? What are your patterns preventing you from achieving?

Exploration: Unravel Your Web

1. What financial, spiritual, mental, relationship (both interpersonal and intrapersonal), and work patterns do you have?
2. Are those patterns serving you?
3. Which pattern or habit have you taken an identity in that when you do not do it feels as if you are no longer yourself?
4. Are there any patterns you would like to change?

Listening to Yourself

As we paddled down the river, there were different sounds— croaking frogs, singing birds, water trickling down the rocks, or a waterfall. These were the different voices and sounds of the river. I wondered whether they cared if anyone listened to them.

Interestingly, we all have an internal conversation, a voice that speaks to us more than it speaks to anyone else. No one is listening to this internal conversation, and we hardly pay attention to it ourselves. What do you say to yourself when no one else is listening? This voice creates a constant chatter, uplifting us or beating us down. The voice, which is sharpened, intimidated, or silenced early in life, continues to pave or block ways for us later in life by telling us what we can or cannot do. It's supported by those emotions from past events or the fear of what could happen. Our self-talk reveals our beliefs, unresolved issues, tail-enders or excuses and fears. Tail-enders are the self-doubts usually linked to any unresolved emotional issue expressed by the voice in your head. The voice is driven by the unconscious mind. Hence, we have to pay attention to it, as it is powerful in creating our reality.

When I started paying attention to my little voice, I realized that I replayed thoughts of anger and at some point planned to avenge the wrongs I thought were done to me. I started tracing where this voice was coming from and realized I had unresolved issues, some as far back as my childhood. I visited the issues to resolve them. I either "pressed refresh," so that I could look at the issues with a different lens, or I accepted that that was the way things were then but that I *am here now*. What I noticed was that this anger from the past actually affected my attitude in the now. I was constantly angry or frowning and was not an easy person to approach or even to get along with. While dealing with my own issues, unaware I punished some people who had no clue what I was dealing with, because of my alienating attitude and behavior toward them. My voice spoke of the past, ignored the present, and wanted to avenge the past in the future. I am sure you can see that I was not living at all.

Your ability to listen to yourself enhances your self-knowledge. This means not only listening to your self-talk but your conversation with others, as both reveal your self-talk in many instances. Most people rehearse a conversation with themselves before they have a conversation with another person. This practice reflects a lot of your unmet needs, values, fears, and beliefs. Learn to pay attention to yourself by listening to yourself talk—a replay of your stored memories that is your subconscious mind.

Exploration: Take Time to Listen to Yourself

1. Take time to listen to yourself for a day. Hear that silent voice that chatters all the time. What do you converse about to yourself? Don't judge it or try to change or fix it; just hear it.

2. Note what the voice says, and explore why you are saying that to yourself.

3. How do you communicate with yourself? Is it in a loving way, loathing way, or judgmental/crucifying way?

4. Is it your own voice, or is it what you have been conditioned to believe? (For example, if someone wrongs you, you expect an apology. This is not your own voice; it's programming.)

5. How does your voice influence your relationships or conversations with others?

Lesson 2

Stay Present

Human mind and news media work on the same principle: unsatisfied with the past; worried about future; ignorant about the present moment.

—Saurabh Sharma

The human brain has a tendency to oscillate between the future and the past and is never in the present. Where do you spend most of your time—in the past or the future? Many people autopilot, live out the beliefs of others and have become a copycat of others. Many never question if what they believe is really are their own belief, if their thoughts are their own, or if their dominant emotions are their own or they have inherited them. Someone who is aware and in the present moment asks these questions. When you ask yourself these questions, you are on a path to reclaiming the power that you may have lost by conforming to the thoughts and beliefs of others. You become free to choose your own set of beliefs and thoughts that direct your inner forces.

Each Moment Makes the Ultimate Plan Come to Pass

> *You must live fully in the now to make your dreams come true.*
> —Florence Scovel Shinn

While we had the day ahead of us planned, and we chose the rapids we would take head-on and the ones we would just watch, the one thing that navigating the river forced us to do was to stay present, surfing or navigating the waves where we were. We could sometimes see how the river was unfolding, but when we went through a rapid, we had to focus on paddling. The thrilling emotions of each rapid could not be taken away by looking at the calmer waters down the river. We could also look back and see the victories we had overcome, but the excitement, challenge, and crisis of each rapid required us to focus so that we could surf and paddle the waves as they came up. When we were present, enjoying the moment-to-moment experiences of the river, there was no stress. Even the fear of upcoming waves was not destructive; it was just there. If we focused on what was to come or what we had done, we would have missed out on each experience as it unfolded.

We have been taught to worry about the future and regret the past. Most people miss opportunities to be happy, to make a difference, or to take a step forward in the direction that could change their lives because they are absent. They are living either in the past, regretting what happened and wondering what could have been, or they are living the future, worrying about what they might need or what could happen in the future. Where do you spend most of your time—past or future? And if you are never in the now, what are you creating? Some people come to the end of their lives and look back with regret at what they did with their years. The challenge is mostly that they did not make the most of *now*.

Staying in the present does not mean you should not plan or anticipate future events. It means you will plan purposefully, being aware when you exit the present to visit the future, to plan and visualize how you would like the future to look. Then you will return to the present to do what you need to do now, to make that manifest. When you visit the past, it will be to resolve or learn. This also means visiting future events and going through all the possible emotions that you could experience, so that when it happens, you are not out of control.

I like what best selling author, teacher and leadership mentor, Dr. Myles Munroe, said in one of his seminars: "I have visited my wife and kids' funeral and experienced all the possible emotions that I could experience." This helps you not to be on autopilot or operate from your programs. You are aware of what is going on. You are not just on a ride without knowing where you are going. To stay in the present, it is essential to train your brain not to stray or to notice when it does and bring it back to reality.

Exploration: Be Here Now and Purposefully Exit

1. Focus your attention on your heartbeat for five minutes (If your mind starts straying, be gentle with yourself, and bring the attention back to your heartbeat.)
2. Purposefully exit (intentional imagine) an event that could happen. Imagine all the possible emotions that you could possibly go through and how you might react or act.
3. How would you like to respond if the event eventually happened?
4. Return to the present, and focus on your heartbeat for five minutes.

Stand Your Reality

The only true thing is what's in front of you right now.
—Ramona Ausubel

Taking each step of the journey and experiencing it made navigating the river worthwhile and gave a sense of tranquility. When we stay in the present, we are able to see things as they are, without trying to quickly escape, deny, or run away from what is. Accepting what is helps to give a sense of peace or acceptance. When we acknowledge what is, sometimes there is no need for fixing anything. We only need to observe and acknowledge that it is what it is. Most people want to quickly escape by fixing, fighting, or judging a challenge that they have not acknowledged or accepted. Mostly, they make a decision that is influenced by an emotion from a past event or by false alarms triggered by their emotional brains. *What is* is the way things are now. See it clearly, without clouding it with judgment.

Each time you do not accept reality the way it is, it will show up as anger, resentment, regret, fear, resistance, revenge, grief, depression, or blame. These negative reactions and emotions take away peace from you. They keep you stuck in the past or have you floating and experiencing future emotions of events and situations that exist only in your mind. When these negatively charged emotions show up, you cannot be fully open, present, and fully accept yourself. So there is an element of self-resentment and self-rejection based on your not accepting your reality. And remember, it's not that you should *not* experience these negatively charged emotions or currents; they are there for a reason, but it's to propel you forward, not to get you stuck. The amount of time you spend on each current or emotion is what matters. While we all process things differently, the aim should be to navigate through negative currents as soon as possible, because your whole life—your mission and purpose—still awaits you. When you have accepted things the way they are, you then can soberly decide and ask yourself questions that can transform your life. Is there still an opportunity to change things and create what you want? What control and power do you have that can change your current reality? If there is nothing you can do to change it, can you change the way you feel about it? Bringing to acceptance *what is* neutralizes the negative emotion and propels you to move forward, as there is no resistance.

Explore Your Reality

1. What is your financial, spiritual, mental, relationship (both interpersonal and intrapersonal), and vocational reality right now?
2. Are you happy with the way things are? If not, is there anything you are to trying run away from? If so, how are you trying to escape?
3. Without wanting to fix, can you be fully present with each situation the way it is and notice the emotions that you experience?
4. Check if your emotions are triggered by a past event or false fear-alarms from the amygdala.

Manage Your Focus and Attention

The present moment is filled with joy and happiness. If you are attentive, you will see it.
—Thích Nhất Hạnh

While navigating the river, we had to focus on each rapid and give it our best shot. When we tipped over, it was still fun, because we knew we had done our best. So we picked ourselves up, and we moved on. It was also joyous and peaceful to see each wave as it came up and disappeared—the continuous flow as a result of a contribution from each wave in the moment. It was easy to get carried away with the waves, but from the information at the beginning of the journey, we knew we had to be highly alert—to pay attention and be present to hear instructions from our guide to either duck, do hard paddle forward or backward, or relax.

This made me realize that we have become busy, mechanical, and automatic to the extent that we cannot see or hear what is around us. Psychologist and author Daniel Goleman said distraction is the new normal. We are distracted on a daily basis by too much information; there is too much to choose from or do. I have watched myself getting distracted—not getting much done and disconnecting from my dear ones or key productive relationships—by moving from one social network to the other, checking my e-mails or my phone. Sometimes I am holding my baby, breastfeeding, chatting on the phone, and trying to respond to an e-mail at the same time. This is not multitasking; it's total distraction. I have observed myself and have asked myself, *What are you doing?*

We get so distracted that we cannot hear a singing bird. We cannot notice our emotions without judging them or quickly wanting to escape. We cannot listen to what our child or partner is saying without being tempted to quickly give an answer without really paying attention. Paying attention in the present moment helps us to notice each emotion as it comes up—its source. It gives us an opportunity to resolve the issue or observe the emotion, and let it go or allow it to flow. So emotions influence our decision making on a daily basis. Whatever we decide to focus on and pay attention to determines what our emotional state will be. Emotions are useful information, telling us how things are around or within us; hence, giving us instructions to move on, relax, or accept what is.

As we let this happen, we do not build up emotions or house them, giving them room to intensify. Staying in the present helps us to bring to acceptance what is, as we cannot always change what is going on. In most cases, if we stay with it instead of trying to escape, we often realize it is not as bad as we thought it was. In the present moment, we also can focus on a particular emotion or event and learn from it by questioning: *why am I feeling the way I am feeling, and what is my responsibility in all this?* We are so engrossed in the busy-ness of our lives that we hardly pay attention to what is going on with our bodies and relationships. We experience emotions in our bodies, and we have to constantly pay attention to the body to get in touch with ourselves. We also pay attention to others each moment and see what is showing up. We have reduced everything to a chore that needs to be accomplished, instead of living the life we ought to live and enjoying each moment. Paying attention heightens self-awareness. Paying attention to the way we speak, eat, walk, listen, or show up allows us to notice *what is* without justifying it. It is in paying attention that we will notice some of our patterns and habits that can be transformed. A gentleman once said to me at a HR conference in Nigeria that you don't need the "you" that is not taking you anywhere.

Sometimes we defend our weaknesses by saying, "That is who I am. Take it or leave it." The "who you are" that destroys good things for you, like quality relationships, can be transformed and enable you to get more of what you want in life, instead of self-sabotaging. It is also in paying attention that you start noticing your inner voice. When you pay attention, noticing what is, there is no contradiction and therefore no internal conflict or resistance. Most conflicts with yourself or with others result from resisting or rejecting what is, and this creates stress and tension in your body. In resisting or rejecting what is, most people engage in behaviors to escape the reality. The decision of what to do is normally clouded by the negative emotions of denial, resentment, and regret. In this case, you end up creating multiple challenges for yourself or even a continuous state of anger, resentment, or bitterness because the problem was not resolved. Focusing and paying attention helps to bring to acceptance what is, before attempting to resolve it or escape. This creates clarity on the issue at hand, and then you can look at alternative solutions.

Stress-Free and Freedom

> *Freedom means you are unobstructed in living your life as*
> *you choose. Anything less is a form of slavery.*
> —Wayne Dyer

If you pay attention to what stresses you, you may see that it is hardly what is happening in the here and now; rather, it is your thoughts of the impact of what is happening, which is what could happen or what has happened. When you stress, you worry about something that might happen in the future or regret something that has happened in the past. The active mind projects a past event or future event into the present. If we focus on the here and now, being with *what is* and not trying to escape or think about what could have been, most of our stress disappears, as we accept what is. Most people are driven by emotions of the past or the future and use those emotions to make decisions about a present situation. You are free if you are not locked up in the past or the future, and you enjoy each present moment. "Living in the moment" does not advocate a lack of planning our lives. We plan the future we want to create, but we remember that it is each moment that makes that plan come to pass.

Past- and future-related emotions prevent you from living your life in the NOW. You are probably living with consequences of choices you made in the past or choices that others made that impacted you. But guess what? Choice is always in the present. Choose again—now. Never give up the power to choose consciously every day, because whatever you choose determines your emotional state, which will inform whether you are stress-free and have freedom. If you choose empowering emotions in the present, like interest, curiosity, optimism, gratitude, joy, cheerfulness, confidence, passion, and determination, you are able to steer yourself up in the direction that solves your challenges and provides you with the solutions you need.

You will know you are obstructed and bound to be stressed if you listen to yourself say, "I would be happier if that had not happened" (past), or "I will be happy if I do, get, or be that" (future). The truth is, you can be happy now by choosing to feel happy despite what is happening. Emotions can be transformed in a split second by understanding how to navigate your internal world, thoughts, and feelings to determine your emotional state. This is not to say we will not experience challenges; we all do. In fact, at any given time, all of us are dealing with some form of challenge, but your emotional state while you have that challenge determines the outcome and what it means to you. It is also your emotional state that determines pain or pleasure and how long you suffer or are free.

Look at the diagram below, and explore why you stress. Check where in time the issue is—past, present, or future. You could say, "I feel sick now; it is a present challenge." But what may stress you about the sickness are your thoughts about what could happen, what you may not be able to do, and what could have caused the sickness. You start projecting the present into the past or future. But if you just focus on where the pain or sickness is and accept what it is, you take away the emotional baggage of the past or future, clearing your energy system and allowing or creating pathways for the body to heal itself.

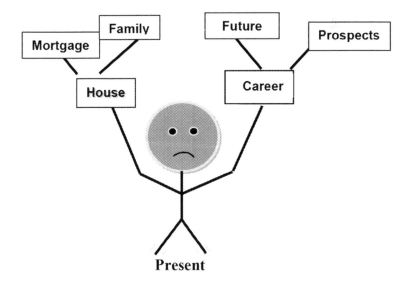

Explore Your Stress: Check In

1. What do you stress about?
2. How do you know you are stressing?
3. When you stress, is the situation or event past, present, or future? (Are you stressed by what is or by what could have been or could be?)
4. What emotions do you experience?
5. If you focus on the here and now, is there anything to stress about?

Lesson 3

Don't Give Power to External Conditions

Don't let the issues outside of your control stop you from addressing issues inside of your control.

—Orrin Woodward

Circumstances, events, other people, and possessions are all external influences of our lives. The internal influence can create any of the external influences depending on the power of the internal force. The external influence cannot steal the power of the internal influence, but the internal influence can surrender its power at times, giving power to external conditions.

The Inside Is More Powerful than the Outside

Nothing splendid has ever been achieved except by those who believed that something inside of them was superior to circumstance.

—Bruce Barton

As we sailed down the river, the gradient was not the same. We had different levels of rapids and some calmer waters. We fell under on some rapids, but we had to quickly get back on the boat and carry on, because the whole river still awaited us. If we rolled over, we had to keep holding on to the security rope until the boat was turned over. The turning over came with challenges for some of us who were not swimmers! We drank a few gallons of water, and this brought some discomfort. Those who lost their grip on the security rope had to float on for a while on their own until the safety boat picked them up. The fear of being on their own was there, but they did not give in. The recovery period was very short, but it was for our own good, to allow us not to get stuck but to keep moving. On class-five rapids, we had to get off the river, walk by the riverside, and carry on the other side, where it was fine for us to paddle. We simply could not afford to give up on our purpose or plan for the day; neither could we submit to the power of the river. It dawned on me that the inflatable boat looked so small compared to the overwhelming sight of the river, with all its rapids and scenic beauty, but it was what was inside that made the boat unsinkable. What was inside was also natural—the air. All that was needed was to tap into it.

Such is the way of life. There are hills, valleys, and mountaintop experiences, each bringing a different set of challenges and lessons. The most challenging for most of us are experiences that are perceived as negative, which we have created or that have been created by others but impact us negatively. Our mastery of our interior power determines how long it takes for us to recover and walk on. Despite what challenges come our way, we have the ability to solve them ourselves.

Your inside is much bigger and more powerful than your outside (remember the iceberg?). If you operate from within, you will be unsinkable, but if you focus on what is outside, the changes and challenges may become overwhelming. Managing emotions for success and happiness requires that you constantly look on the inside.

Most of us, though, have been trained, conditioned, and educated to look on the outside when making decisions or to rely on the outside to be happy. We are also schooled that we have nothing on the inside, so we need to get what is outside to fill the inside. As such, we try to look on the outside to appease the inside, and in most cases we create disharmony, unhappiness, bitterness, and failure. Looking from the inside out allows you to become congruent, forceful, and unsinkable. The challenges on the outside include creating fulfilling relationships; creating a fulfilling life, financially, spiritually, morally, and mentally; and adapting to the changing world. If you can manage your emotions—that is, choose to respond and focus on the inside instead of reacting and focusing on the outside—you will find fulfillment. François de la Rochefoucauld, a noted French author said, "When we are unable to find tranquility within ourselves, it is useless to seek it elsewhere."

Manage Your Conduct Purposefully

> *Circumstances are beyond human control, but our condition, but our conduct is in our own power.*
> —Benjamin Disraeli

When external conditions present challenges, when we do not feel great about ourselves, or when we do not accept the way things are, we have the power to choose our behavior to create the outcomes we want. Most often, however, when we are triggered or faced with challenges, we react, giving away power to the external condition. When we manage our conduct purposefully we choose behaviors that get the results we want, and we remain responsible for the condition we are in. Our condition is how we feel about what has taken place and how we have handled it. In any given circumstance, we get stuck or experience negative emotions when we fail to manage our conduct—that is, choose a behavior and a positive emotion that keep us flowing.

A family member with whom I just had a chat is a typical example. She spoke about how bitter and angry she is with her late father (gone for a couple of years) for being abusive to her mother, her siblings, and her. She even shed tears. I felt her pain and even experienced an emotion of hurt, but I quickly snapped out of it and went into assessment. In assessing, my thoughts were that she had no control over his behavior. No one has control over anyone's actions, yet she still suffers emotionally for his behavior, punishing herself for other people's behavior. However, she has power over her condition—that is, what she feels on the inside about it and her conduct and what she decides to do moving forward to create what she would like, not what happened. She also acknowledged that she fears having that in her life; hence, her conduct now with the opposite sex is based on fear, not trust or love.

The question I always ask is, who should suffer: the person who acted badly or the one to whom the behavior or action was done? I know now that the person who behaved or acted in a manner that hurt others' feelings or hurt them physically must suffer, not by my wanting revenge but by the laws of the universe. The law of cause and effect tells us that we cannot do something negative and expect a positive result—this is where karma comes from. Society teaches us to suffer for other people's behavior, and by doing so, we give away power to external conditions. We bring the outside on the inside and create a victim—a revenge or blame mentality, which allows what is on the outside to create disharmony on the inside, ultimately creating more challenges on the outside.

Circumstances can help you to create your values or clarify your values (what is important to you), and then channel your energy to what is important to you. This is managing your conduct purposefully. You are aware of what is important to you and choose behaviors that result in those outcomes, even if it means temporary discomfort. For some, circumstances create an opportunity to become more self-destructive by destroying your values, denying your values, and derailing the results you want by channeling energy to what is not important and getting stuck in revenge, bitterness, blame, grief, and loathing. These negative emotions create an attitude in you that can make you say what you do not mean, causing a loss of or damage to a relationship. There is no useful purpose and value in these negative conditions. While you may find yourself there, remember that how long you stay there matters, because the longer you stay there, the longer you stay unfulfilled, and you are not flowing.

The conscious awareness questions to manage your conduct purposefully are to continually ask yourself: what are you creating?; what are you focusing on?; what are you channeling your energy on?: and does this enhance your flow? This allows you to respond— to enhance your ability to respond to any given circumstance and align the inside to what is outside.

Exploration: Assess the Circumstance

1. What opportunities are there in the challenge, if you manage to resolve it purposefully?
2. Is it temporary or permanent?
3. What story are you telling yourself about it, and what beliefs are running in your head about how it should be, as opposed to just seeing things the way they are?
4. What fears, unmet needs, values, and beliefs are revealed by the story?
5. Is it possible that you have been making this event bigger or smaller than it is?
6. What action will be purposeful in this event?

Lesson 4

Adapt Purposefully

The only thing constant in life is change.
—François de la Rochefoucauld

Be Aware of Change

It was interesting to note that the river was not constant. The gradient kept changing, and the rapids were not the same; hence, we constantly had to adapt our action or behavior to the ongoing changes. Some change we initiated, like avoiding the big rapids and taking a swim in the calm waters, and some change we did not ask for, like getting an unexpected swim while going through a rapid, or getting stuck on an obstruction, or even finding ourselves on our own, floating down the river, waiting to be rescued. At times, we just had to hang on the security rope for us not to be thrown out by the turbulence and ride through. Other times, we had to let go of the security rope to begin to paddle again or not even paddle at all. Change is guaranteed, and what we require is wisdom to embrace change. Charles Darwin said, *"It is not the strongest of the species that survives, nor the most intelligent but one most responsive to change."*

We are living in times of rapid change, isolation, and complexity. Each time you experience an emotional turbulence or some form of discomfort, it shows that there is change going on. You need to adapt. Many do not want to experience discomfort; hence, they quickly escape and instead of seeing and accepting the change, they engage in behaviors that give temporary comfort or act as a tranquilizer, such as drinking alcohol, becoming a villain, smoking, indulging in sex with multiple partners, divorce, and more. These actions are neither wrong nor right. The question is, are they helping you to adapt to what is changing in a manner that helps you to be you, or do they make you feel your best? What future are you creating? If you stepped into the future, would you be happy if you looked at what you created?

Emotional Freedom Technique (EFT) Founder, Gary Graig indicates that many addictions are born out of people who have failed to manage negative emotions purposefully. The root cause of addictions could be anxiety, anger, guilt, and blame, and sufferers adapt in a negative way. The challenge is, whatever action you may take in trying to adapt to change and think is temporary, it contributes to building your future. Failure to see the whole picture as you adapt to change can create more discomfort or unwanted change in the future. For example, you end up in a relationship that makes you very unhappy because when you saw the signs—that this did not align with your values—you feared change, and you carried on. You ended up with a job that made you unhappy. You ended up broke, you ended up depressed or bitter, you ended up sick, you became an addict, or you ended up stuck. You are not getting the results you want.

Go Inside

> *The reasonable man adapts himself to the world; the unreasonable one persists in trying to adapt the world to himself. Therefore all progress depends on the unreasonable man.*
>
> —George Bernard Shaw

When adapting to change, you have to identify, experience, and understand the emotions of change, both positive and negative.

If you experience negative emotions, which is the case for most people, identify the emotion to transform it, or to be with it until a positive emotion kicks in, or you are used to the change phase. Change brings with it uncertainties, so it is normal to feel afraid or to try to escape. Most personal change efforts or change in organizations fail because the focus is on the outside (behaviors) and not the drivers of behaviors (emotions). To create lasting change, emotions must be transformed from negative to positive, and then, adapting to change will be automatic.

Once you are aware of what you feel, you can question how to use what is happening to align more with your talents and values. How can you leverage your key strengths to resolve the challenge? Align what is happening to your purpose or your core. Sometimes, it is your expectations of how things should transpire playing with you, rather than what is actually happening. I remember one situation when I thought I was having it rough. I had just graduated with a master's degree, relocated to a new country, was seven months pregnant, and single. After I had my baby, it took me six months to get a job. My savings had run out, and depending on friends was very painful. I got a job as a conference producer, a job I had to take out of sheer desperation. Once in that position, I realized that most of my peers did not even have a bachelor's degree. Even my boss at the time was working on her bachelor's degree at the University of South Africa through distance learning.

I had high expectations of what the world should give because of what I had acquired. I drifted into negativity, even loathing. I hated my job and was bitter with everyone around me. But something inside of me kicked in, and I realized that while I expected better, no one owed me anything and if I expected better no one would just hand it to me but I had to create it. Therefore, I did not have to play the victim. If I wanted something different, I had to make my way towards it. John Maxwell, one of the leadership gurus, said if you do not go within, you will go without. When faced with a challenge, ask yourself, how do I maintain my own integrity here?

Live out your values and therefore align what is happening to ensure the outcome is aligned to what is important to you. The inside is full; the 91 percent of the iceberg is on the inside and the external is 9 percent, which is your behavior. Your choice of response to change must fill up the 91 percent so that you have 100 percent fulfillment. Your external world connects with your internal world. To adapt to change by going inside, ask yourself how you can align what is happening to your values, traits, image, and motives. Change what is on the outside, such as behavior and beliefs, to align within to fulfill your values.

Initiate Change Purposefully

While you cannot change everything, you can change how you feel about certain things that you cannot change. Many leave a lot to fate and go on the journey of life without purposefully deciding what is it they want to create with their lives. You may say you want money, and you are able to make the money, but if your purpose is unclear, you will spend the money on things that still leave you unfulfilled. When you are clear about the legacy you want to create, you can initiate change purposefully by choosing the situations you would like and constantly checking your compass to see if you are still in the right direction. You can initiate change to ensure that you continue to aim toward your goals. When you initiate change, you can give yourself a command and keep it. You are also prepared to go through the change, riding the biggest waves skillfully, like an experienced kayaker going through the biggest rapid. Dare to be different. Initiate change. When you initiate change, you have to express your uniqueness. Your uniqueness can come only on the inside and can be experienced on the outside.

When you initiate change, you create a powerful emotional state of curiosity and inspiration that moves you to create a whole new world for you. Author and founder of EFT, Gary Craig, in his book *The Palace of Possibilities*, mentions that we all live in a palace of possibilities with many rooms in it, but most of us live in the dungeon or only in one room of that palace. This is because we do not initiate change; we do not step out to check what is in the other rooms—we don't step out to possibilities. If you do not initiate change in your life, chances are you are locked up in conformity, passivity, total distraction, and complacency.

Accept Change

> *Acceptance is not a state of passivity or inaction.*
> —Peter McWilliams

Acceptance does not mean conformity, submission, or complacency. It means acknowledging what is going on and then deciding on a course of action. People conform more to their beliefs about the change than to the change itself. When inevitable change, like the loss of a loved one, happens, there are beliefs that you have to worry and grieve to show that you have experienced loss. If you do not worry and grieve, it shows that you do not care. In assessing my own beliefs about death, I realized that I have been socialized to believe that when there is a death in the community, neighbors and community members all cry. The question I have asked myself lately is, why do I cry? I am not saying we should not cry, but most of us are on autopilot, or we revert to a common ritual and conformity—the way it has always been done. This, for me, is really not acceptance. Acceptance says, this is what is happening. I am in touch with my reality. Then I start questioning what this means for me and what I should do with it.

Any loss is followed by emotions of sadness and grief. While you can go through the emotional wave of loss, how much time you spend in the center, which is grief, matters. The longer you stay, the longer you have not accepted change. It's as if you are saying to yourself, "I cannot live without …" whatever you have lost—money, a job, a relationship, or a loved one. Going back to questioning emotions, remember that when we lose most attachments we have developed, it may feel like we cannot live without them, but the truth is that we can live on. Going through the emotional wave and developing other negative emotions, like anger and bitterness, means we are in denial of the change and getting stuck. While crying and venting are means of letting out the emotion and can assist in adapting to change, all you need to remember is that it should not be forever—do not get stuck.

My new belief for loss is that I must celebrate the opportunity, time spent, and the life lived, in case of death. I have also had regrets on how I could have done better but then realized that I can do better going forward, not backward—I have learned that from the change of loss. It is also easy to get stuck in blame when change happens, instead of taking individual responsibility—that is, you can choose to get stuck or keep flowing on your journey by the emotions you experience. When you are dominated by negative emotions, ask yourself what change you are struggling to accept. What beliefs or expectations are contributing to the struggle to accept or are triggering your survival instincts? You cannot change what you have not accepted. Expectations can cause you to build an ego wall of pride and arrogance, and these can prevent you from accepting change or initiating change. The ego wall also can prevent you from reaching on the inside for your essence and what is truly important to you, so that you can manage your contact purposefully.

Depersonalize Change

> *Never build a case against yourself.*
> —Robert Rowbottom

We are socialized to own or possess, and encouraged to keep acquiring possessions, so that we own. There is a misconception that when we own more, we will feel better. How many things do you own that you call yours? Your car, your house, your spouse, your children, your church, your religion, your team—the list is endless. While owning is neither bad or good, it is the change of ownership through a shift or movement that create a turbulence. As the change happens which could be loss of anything you have owned or attached to yourself you feel like you have lost a part of who you are, and hence personalize change.

Most people would rather not lose anything. Even when the loss is inevitable, like death, they would rather not think about it, or they live as if it will never happen. When it eventually does happen, it throws them out of balance. People would rather live with the hope of not losing something than have certainty that they will lose something. This loss aversion makes adapting to change a challenge, and it makes initiating change a challenge. They own certain rituals, habits, and patterns. Shifting them, transforming them, or getting rid of them can make these people feel discomfort. They would rather carry on with the security of what they know.

The phrase "this is who I am" means that I own my behaviors, habits, and patterns, and even if they are sabotaging me, I do not want to lose them. When change occurs, do not make it about your identity; rather, make it about how you can respond and see it as a challenge. When you focus on how you can respond, you are saying you can alter or change your behavior. You can transform your emotions. You can change your patterns or habits. You can reframe how you see things. You can give what is happening or has happened a new meaning by upgrading your belief system. If you do not upgrade or update your system, it will crash.

Change occurs to everyone at any given point in time. Every one of us is going through some change. When you personalize change or make it about you, you choose to punish yourself for the inevitable, which is change. When you build a case against yourself, it is self-sabotaging and disempowering. When you build a case for yourself, you activate the self-belief to keep moving on.

Change Your Story

> *We tell ourselves stories in order to live.*
> —Joan Didion

Stories are what keep us going. At any given point, we are running a script of a story about what is happening, what has happened, or what should happen. There is normally a gap between what is happening and what should happen. That gap shapes the story you end up with, whether there is a problem or a challenge or whether you are doomed or excited. If you check the way you speak about the change—the language you use—you will know if you are aware of change, can initiate change, or have accepted change. Are you telling a victim or victor story? A blame or responsible story? A failure or success story? A hopeful or hopeless story? Does the story reflect your going inside or outside for solutions? If your story is keeping you stuck, refresh the perspective, or change the frame or context in which you evaluate and interpret what is happening.

Stories run our lives. Your results today tell you the quality of your story or the quality of others' stories you have been following. It is usually others' stories that influence what you end up believing about love, lifestyle, money, fame, and so on. Often, our stories run on autopilot and are driven by what we fear, rather than by what inspires us. Instead of singling out a story or a few stories with the results you want to model, you will record all the stories with warning signs that make change difficult. Open your story case and check what scripts you have about money, love, work, success. How does that story make you feel? Your story confirms or determines your self-concept.

Create your own story, not by reinventing the wheel but by modeling the results of people who inspire you. Don't run or rerun scripts of people with results that scare you. Sometimes your story may be distorted by others' stories about you, and this may destroy your confidence or self-worth, if you believe their story of you instead of your story about yourself. Your stories always have a reference point—an anchor. This anchor is the beliefs you have developed from your experiences and events that have shaped your life. When change occurs, people often look at information that can validate or confirm those beliefs, instead of acknowledging what is going on. Hence, one might end up with a distorted story.

Get Help

> *Good friends help you to find important things when you*
> *have lost them ... your smile, your hope, your courage.*
> —Doe Zantamata

Sometimes change can be overwhelming, especially if it is unexpected. Run to get help, and tell someone you trust or someone who will listen. There are times in life when we all need to share our burdens with a friend. It helps to find relief while we go through transition or go through the motions of change. Getting help or sharing the challenges or difficulty with others creates an opportunity for a fresh perspective from someone who is not experiencing the strong emotions that can impair thinking. Getting help can help us to adapt to change sometimes, instead of denying or resisting change. Remember, each time we feel some form of discomfort, change is happening.

Lesson 5

Have Some Options and Tools

There are many ways of going forward but only one way of standing still.

—Franklin D. Roosevelt

We had tools for the journey: water to avoid dehydration, safety jackets, safety boats for rescue, professional kayakers to help challenging situations, professional photographers, and food (pineapples and cookies, helmets in case we fell on the rocks, throw-bags for rescuing someone, and a first-aid kit. We prepared for all the possible outcomes for the day by anticipating what could happen. Preparing helped us to transform fear into courage. If we had not anticipated possible occurrences and prepared for them, it would have been easy to get stuck by concentrating on one possible outcome, which would be a smooth excursion.

Before we set out, we could choose what sort of day we wanted and who we wanted to spend the day with. We had choices, but we had to make a decision. Not everyone, however, consciously made a decision. I noticed some individuals just jumped into any boat. This means that they ended up with an experience that they did not want. At the end of the journey, some said, "I should have come with you." They did not plan what they wanted and therefore did not make a choice purposefully. Along the way, we deliberately avoided big rapids—we took a walk alongside the river to pass this situation and then we got back on the river again.

We have been conditioned from our formal and informal education system to believe that in most situations, there is only one solution to the challenge and that socially, there is only one way we must feel if a certain event occurs. For example, in most cultures, there is a belief that when you lose a loved one, you should grieve; if someone betrays you, you must feel hurt or angry; or if you perceive someone as better than you, you should put that person on a pedestal, feel jealousy, or admire him or her in a way that says you cannot become your best. The brain is then wired to constantly see one way to resolve a challenge—or worse, even call it a "problem." so the focus becomes the problem, not the possible solution.

Psychologists and authors MacNair and Elliott indicated that problem-solving abilities are significantly reduced by stress. When faced with a challenging situation, it is easy to stress and engage in your survival mode; this is "fight or flight." It is difficult to solve challenges when you are in this state or to creatively generate options and weigh them to select the best with the outcome, as you experience a diminishing focus. It is easy to think there is no way out if you focus on the problem instead of focusing on finding a way out. Remember what Gary Craig, the founder of the emotional freedom technique (EFT), said we live in a "palace of possibilities," but many of us are stuck in one room of that palace. Some have never stepped out of that room.

I used to get stuck because I grew up with a subconscious belief that the answer is always one solution to a problem; I was stuck in one room. So each time I had a challenge, my brain was locked up by wanting to see that solution that I had pre-planned, instead of asking myself what else I could do to solve this challenge or resolve the problem. But the moment I learned that for any challenge, there is more than one solution, life became exciting. With any challenge that I face now, I ask myself what options I have. The result is always tremendous, always a way out. The more options you have, the better choices you can make.

Prepare the Toolbox

Nobody ever wrote a plan to be broke, fat, lazy, or stupid.
Those things are what happen when you don't have a plan.
—Larry Winget

No one hands you a toolbox that is full of options to deal with the challenges you encounter in life. Hence, most people live by chance. They walk around with an empty case, without a plan to handle challenges. They come up with survival strategies at their point of weakness, which is when threatened with challenges. Chances of coming up with a purposeful plan in this state are significantly reduced, as you experience a diminishing focus. Bear in mind that your options and tools must be purposeful; that means, give life instead of destroying it. If you want to put together a toolbox of different ways to commit suicide by engaging in destructive behaviors, then you need to revisit your plan. The options must be informed by the awareness that emotions influence our results by influencing our actions and inactions—what we do or don't do.

To prepare your toolbox, you need to have a plan in place. If you do not have a plan, it becomes difficult to put together a toolbox. What do you want to achieve? A toolbox is useful for problem solving. Many walk around with an empty toolbox or one option (one tool), resulting in their always panicking, getting angry or disappointed, or relying on survival modes when the "tool" does not deliver. Have more than one way for things to be perfect. You can help to build stability and balance by anticipating challenging future events and preparing the different types of emotions and behavior in which to engage. Having tools and exercising options-thinking helps you to see, create, and evaluate options. This is critical for problem solving and also to manage negativity. Using a toolbox with a lot of tools and options requires flexibility. Some people have the tools but are stuck with one way of doing things—patterns, beliefs, and habits. What are you storing in your toolbox to help you navigate the rapids and waves of life? Most individuals who are successful in managing emotions exercise options-thinking, and that helps them to navigate emotions. Having the options (tools) to manage emotions is a self-regulation or self-management technique.

Emotions are generated in a five-step process:

1. You start with a situation, which might be real or imagined.
2. You focus your attention on this situation.
3. You give the situation meaning by evaluating or interpreting it.
4. This makes you feel a certain way.
5. You behave a certain way, which is your response or reaction.

By expanding your awareness on these five steps, you can facilitate or generate positive emotions. Our options to manage emotions successfully must look at addressing these five steps to facilitate or generate positive useful emotions:

1. Situation
2. Focusing attention

3. Interpretation or evaluation
4. Emotions
5. Behavior—your response

Choosing Your Situations

If you choose your situations purposefully, you may be able to handle to the emotions that come with them. The primary focus must shift from dealing with negative situations to preventing them. Setting your goals, defining your purpose, planning, and setting your personal vision is part of situation selection. It also sets boundaries on what you want to experience in your life as a person. What do you want out of life? If situations show up that are contrary to or deviate from your planned situations, you can modify or change them, knowing full well what you want to experience. If you cannot change or modify the situation, take yourself out of situations that constantly make you feel negative, because they are not aligned to what is important to you. Avoiding and disengaging from a negative situation can be a way of selecting your situation. Remember, choice can be voluntary or involuntary—either way, you are choosing.

If you do not have a plan, you will end up in a particular situation and wonder how you got there. Leaving a lot to fate can leave you in a reactionary state or survival mode most of the time. While there are situations over which you have no control, which are laws of the universe or the nature of life, like knowing that everything is in transition and constantly evolving, you can sharpen your skills to adapt by exercising and flexing your emotional muscles. In looking at the key areas you want to fulfill, what situations do you have in your relationships at work, with family, with friends, financially, with God or a higher being, or with yourself, mentally and physically? Everything adds up to relationships. What relationship do you choose or plan to have with money? Is it transactional, indebtedness, or overflow? What relationship do you have with yourself? Do you practice enough self-care, mentally, spiritually, and physically? What situations would you like? What plan do you have or do you have to make? What goals do you need to set? Who is going to make you accountable?

Focusing Your Attention

Are you able to notice what you focus your attention in a given situation? Do you focus on the positive or the negative? Do you focus on what you can change or cannot change, or on what you have control over or what you do not? Are you able to move your attention from the negative to the positive, from what you cannot change to what you can change? Wherever you focus your attention, energy goes there, and that means the situation will grow or expand. For example, you may focus on the opportunity to give a speech and make a good impression, as opposed to focusing on worrying about making a bad impression. When you focus on the negative energy, that situation is wasted.

Reframing

The meaning we give a situation through interpretation and evaluation makes us feel a certain way. What meaning do you give to your relationships? Are you caged, satisfied, or excited? The same situation can make two people feel differently due to the different interpretation. You give meaning through your thought process, most of the time subconsciously, using stored information from past events. However, if you do not update your memory regularly, most of your information may be outdated or linked to a totally different situation than what you have at hand. Your belief and value system that has developed through your life experiences are not global and cannot be generalized to every situation that happen in your life. If your interpretation of a situation keeps you stuck, give the situation new meaning—that is, reframe it.

Reframing helps you to update your memory by changing your thoughts about a given situation, choosing to expand your perspective, and stepping into the "palace of possibilities," instead of being stuck in one room.

You could ask yourself questions to reframe; such as, what valuable lessons could I learn from this situation, or how else could I look at this? You could also ask someone who is not emotionally attached to the event or situation to interpret it, thus distancing yourself from the situation. Having a sense of humor can give a situation new meaning or make you see things differently. Changing your belief system also can assist you to reframe; by adopting a new belief system, you see things differently.

Transforming and Releasing Emotion

> *A man who is a master of himself can end a sorrow as easily as he can invent a pleasure. I don't want to be at the mercy of my emotions. I want to use them, to enjoy them and to dominate them.*
>
> —Oscar Wilde

What are your dominant emotions? Are you able to recognize and name these emotions as they come from each situation? Using the questioning techniques (found in the discussion on emotional literacy), you can transform emotions or facilitate positive emotions. You need to hold on to positive emotions and let go of negative emotions, remembering that each emotion has a maximum lifespan of 120 seconds. Each time you continue to feel something after two minutes, it is a choice. You are choosing to harbor or hoard the negative emotions. You may say it is not easy, and when you say that your brain shuts off trying to release the emotion, resisting what is possible or what could happen. Would you rather say, "I will try to improve my life"? This way, you are now open to possibilities. Question the negative emotion and burn it out. Some of the techniques used to release emotions include exercising, which helps you to burn the negatively charged electro-chemical signal from your bloodstream; and the emotional freedom technique (EFT), also known as tapping. EFT is a tool to release negatively charged emotions. Tapping uses acupressure points—it's like acupuncture without needles. Tapping uses the meridian points, repeating a setup statement or a reminder phrase for the emotion you are experiencing. It usually releases the emotion in minutes. To learn more about this technique, visit my website: mavismazhura.com.

ABC's of Behavior

> *When obstacles arise, you change your direction to reach*
> *your goal; you do not change your decision to get there.*
> —Zig Ziglar

Greek philosopher Epictetus said, *"It is not what happens to you but how you react to it that matters."* You cannot choose some situations, but you can choose your response. When you find yourself in a challenging situation, are you able to assess the situation—the present and future impact? Do you evaluate various options to respond to the situation with the outcome in mind, and then borrow a behavior and contact your behavior purposefully? Borrowing a behavior is when you do something that is not natural to you to get certain results. Do you realize that most of the time when you experience negatively charged emotions and your survival instincts are triggered, your behavior takes you away from your goal? Negative emotions signal a threat; hence, people may avoid the situation or engage in the fight-or-flight mode, reducing chances to reach the goal or achieve the outcome they want. Engaging a different behavior than the one that gets you stuck, which is known as borrowing a behavior, can help you to change how you feel, as well as the results thereof. Asking yourself what you could do differently helps you to generate the different options of behaviors. In any given situation, follow the ABC's:

- Assess the situation and the different ways of behaving.
- Borrow a behavior.
- Conduct a behavior to reach your goal.

Lesson 6

Team Up with People Who have created or are creating the Results You Want

If you hang out with chickens, you're going to cluck, and if you hang out with eagles, you're going to fly.
— Steve Maraboli

© Dziewul | Dreamstime.com

We had to work as a team when river rafting and chose the team with which we wanted to work. No one had to paddle alone. Getting on the boat with the right people—those who wanted to create the same outcomes—was essential for creating the results we wanted. It was the teammates who brought us back in if we found ourselves taking an unplanned swim. It was the teammates who held us accountable for our paddling. We had an expert guide who made our life easier by telling us what worked in the high waters, to the extent that some of us who had never been on a raft knew how to do it. He was our role model for the day. When we did not know what to do, we looked to him.

People are the biggest resource and whether we are aware of it or not, we are influenced by the people with whom we surround ourselves, whether it is through music, books, movies, or the food we eat. Our results are affected either positively or negatively by what we surround ourselves with. We will use some of the phrases those people use and behave like them sometimes. Our tastes may even be influenced by them.

If you do not have a plan, you will go with the crowd. If you have a plan but surround yourself with people or things that do not flow in the same direction as you, you may experience friction and internal conflict. It might also take longer to get your results, because no one holds you accountable. You may read a book or listen to an audiotape, but those things will not hold you accountable. Other people will hold you accountable and push you to achieve your maximum potential.

Modeling

> *If I have seen farther than others, it is because I was standing on the shoulders of giants.*
>
> —Isaac Newton

I ask people in our Emotional Intelligence course to name their role models, some often respond, "Myself," or "I have no role model," or "I do not want to be disappointed when those people behave in a way contrary to my expectations." This shows how some people are unaware that someone is influencing them involuntarily. We learn through modeling, aware or unaware. Intentional modeling gives us an opportunity to choose, intentionally and purposefully, someone with the results we want and to identify their patterns of success and emulate them. This helps to generate positive emotions of curiosity, interest, and optimism, learning from their successes and their failures and how they responded to challenging situations. Remember, role models do not have to be perfect; they are human, like you and me, so choose what you want to focus on to your own benefit.

Check your relationships. Who has the relationship with money that you would want to create? Who has a marriage that you would want to create? Who has wisdom that you would to create? Who has physical fitness that you would want to create? What are their patterns? Model the patterns, so you do not have to start from scratch.

Coach/Mentor or Teacher

To be successful in any area, you have to learn as much as you can about it. Learn the rules and the science behind any area you want to fulfill. We live in a world bombarded with information and so many distractions, so that if no one holds you accountable, you will abandon your dream and your goal and get stuck in habits and patterns that do not serve you. A coach/mentor helps you to achieve results faster by holding you accountable and helps you to condition your mind and emotions to new states that can move you toward your goals. A coach/mentor will help you to expand your awareness, figuring out what is not working and creating new ways. Your coach/mentor is an expert guide who will remind you of what to do when you are stuck. He or she is your sounding board and accountability partner. Get a coach/mentor who can get you on track and kick your butt to keep moving. If you already have one, then great, but remember that different areas of your life may require a different mentor. Most successful people have a coach/mentor. Learning from the best teachers gets you on the path to success. Who are your teachers? I do not only read from my great teachers; I have met some of them. When I do, one of my dreams or goals is accomplished, and I feel great.

Cheerleaders

Cheerleaders are people who believe in you and your strength, and even if they are not creating similar results as you, they believe in your results. They will support you and give you words of encouragement to keep you going. If you surround yourself with people who are always trying to put you down or who give you destructive criticism, you may have challenges in reaching your goals. You may experience low self-esteem, low self-belief, and compromised self-confidence. At one point as I was writing this book, my husband asked me if I had finished it. Because I had failed to make time to do so, I was a bit irate. I asked him why he didn't write one himself and see how challenging it is. He said that he did not have the skills to write a book, but he believed I did, and therefore, I must complete the book—there were many people waiting for the book who would benefit from it. What an amazing man! He believes in me. He believes in my strength and my success, even when I do not. From that moment, I felt that I owed him the completion of this book for his giving me such encouragement. He never stopped asking when I was going to finish. He steered positive emotions of determination, courage, hope, and self-confidence my way. I would do my friends an injustice if I did not acknowledge their support as well. Who facilitates the generation of positive ideas and emotions around you? It could be friends, your children, siblings, or colleagues at work. Whoever they are, do not let them down.

Lesson 7

Don't Flow Back on Yourself: Get Out of Obstructions as Soon as Possible— Your Whole Life Still Awaits You

As I walked out the door toward my freedom, I knew that if I did not leave all the anger, hatred, and bitterness behind that I would still be in prison.

—Nelson Mandela

As we carried on along the river, a safety boat got stuck. It had food, water, and safety-aid kits on it. All the other boats had to wait for him to get off. The guide struggled, to the point that another safety boat had to paddle back upstream to rescue him, and because he was going against the current, the journey up was not easy. When he got there, he let lose the bags, as they were anchoring the rope in the wrong direction, and then he threw a rope to pull the other boat. Our expert guide explained that he was stuck on an obstruction, or an eddy. At this point, water flows back on itself instead of flowing forward. He had to get unstuck, as the whole river awaited us.

I looked up in Wikipedia what an obstruction is, and this is what I got:

> Obstruction: A boulder or ledge in the middle of a river or near the side can obstruct the flow of the river, and can also create a "pillow"; when water flows backwards upstream of the obstruction, or a "pour over" (over the boulder); and "hydraulics" or "holes" where the river flows back on itself—perhaps back under the drop—often with fearful results for those caught in its grasp. (Holes, or hydraulics, are so-called because their foamy, aerated water provides less buoyancy and can feel like an actual hole in the river surface.) If the flow passes next to the obstruction, an eddy may form behind the obstruction; although eddies are typically sheltered areas where boaters can stop to rest, scout or leave the main current, they may be swirling and whirlpool-like.

We know that flow is our default state of being, and we flow when we experience positively charged emotions. However, sometimes we face obstacles on our journey that cause us to experience negatively charged emotions—such is the nature of life. Certain changes or transitions can cause discomfort as well. While this is relatively normal, the challenge comes when we harbor negatively charged emotions, as they then find somewhere to settle in our bodies. When negative emotions settle, they disrupt the body's natural way of eliminating impurities from the body. In fact, the negative emotions add to the impurities in the system. The result as mentioned before, is feeling unwell, emotionally and/ or physically, and in some instances, giving rise to dis-ease, either immediately or in the long run. You release stress hormones, like cortisol and adrenaline, to prepare you for action. However, even though you have been triggered for action and you end up doing nothing, the stress hormones drain your body of energy, causing fatigue. Conversely, extreme tiredness and fatigue can cause stress. You may find yourself caught up in a vicious cycle of stress and fatigue. And when this happens, you will find yourself taking longer to accomplish your goals, feeling irritable, procrastinating, or simply stuck in a pattern to get by and without creativity. If you have an unresolved emotional issue, you may experience headaches, heartaches, memory failure, stress, low energy, lack of achievement, difficulty making decisions, depression, being dependent on medicinal drugs, suicidal thoughts, conflict, social phobia, relationship challenges, low self-esteem, lack of confidence, constant fear of death, shyness and embarrassment, emotional eating, skin problems, and gaining weight, among many others.

I have called the state where you hold on to negatively charged emotions that result in any undesirable state "flowing back on yourself." When "flow back on yourself", the journey is not easy. You are continuously sending the same signal to the brain to release the same electro-chemical signal, as though the event is happening continuously. And even if the event is recurring because your survival signals are alert, you do not have the resources (that is, healthy emotions) to diffuse the situation or create a solution. Some people have the skill of diffusing a negative event with ease—this is because they have healthy emotions. Negative emotions are an obstruction, blocking you from your desired results. Negative emotions and thoughts will anchor you in the wrong direction and keep you walled in one spot. If not released, they can immobilize you permanently.

Emotions and Behaviors of Obstruction

> *You can't change what's going on around you until you start changing what's going on within you.*
> —Zig Ziglar

What are your dominant emotions? You are what you are on the inside, meaning that your behavior on the outside is influenced by how you feel inside. If you experience a dominant feeling of fear, you may express inaction, avoidance, postponement, indecision, aggression, manipulation or defensiveness. Remember, negative emotions come as a result of a situation that we interpret as negative or positive, and the situation can be real or imagined. If you decide to focus on the negative for a prolonged time, you will start flowing back on yourself. The brain does not know whether the situation is occurring, has occurred, or will occur. The same electro-chemical signal is released as if it is happening now. The two fundamental emotions we are born with are love and fear. All the other emotions emanate from these two. We experience fear and love within us; we feel these emotions, and they are our divine nature.

Since we are born with two fears—fear of falling and fear of a loud noise—then what remains is love. If we express it as a percentage, 98 percent of who we are is love, and 2 percent is fear. Fear is there for survival, in case of real threats. For example, seeing a lion fear will trigger the release of hormones that energize the fight-or-flight response. If fear is only 2 percent of our divine nature, it should have rare occurrences in our lives, and transforming the fear should be easy, given that 98 percent of our nature is love. Fear triggers the survival instinct or the stress response to prepare you for action. The challenge, though, is that real danger is rare, but our habits of life trigger the survival instinct, even where there is no life-or-death threat. Hence, continuous release of negative electro-chemical signals into your bloodstream weakens the immune system—the body's natural way of restoring itself. If the stress hormones released during the stressful situation remain in the bloodstream, it gives rise to self-poisoning, and every cell in the body is affected, giving rise to disease.

Think about how many hours of your day you spend dominated by thoughts and emotions of fear, as opposed to emotions of love? Most people are out of balance, dominated by 98 percent fear and 2 percent love. Emotions emanating from fear that may trigger the survival instinct emotions which include anger, boredom, sadness, and guilt. In fact, all the negative emotions show some aspect of fear. If you knew and believed that whatever happens does not matter, you would not experience the negatively charged emotions for an extended period.

Emotions emanating from love, on the other hand, include trust, acceptance, interest, happy, joy, serenity, and hope, and again, all the positive emotions show an aspect of love.When we experience emotions of fear dominantly, we get stuck. This affects our story, focus, state, energy levels, and consequently, results.

Let's explore the most common and dominant emotions of obstruction, which are in the family of fear that show flowing back on yourself.

Anger is always a secondary emotion, which shows that there is a fear and triggers the fight or flight stress response mechanism. Reaction to anger can be destructive and response to anger is constructive. However, before you feel angry, you feel something else first. It could be annoyance, disgust, apprehension, fear, or anticipation. So when you feel angry, you are already flowing back on yourself, because you have allowed the primary emotion to intensify from a low-energy emotion, whether you are aware or unaware. What matters, however, is the length of time you spend feeling angry. If you are able to recognize the low energy emotion and transform it, you get back in the flow quickly. The flight expression of anger can be passive behavior, and the fight can be aggressive behavior. Passive behaviors can show up as gossip, self-sabotaging behaviors, addictions, a victim mentality or self-pity, self-criticism, selfishness, bitterness, resentment, hatred, blame, and many others. Aggressive behaviors can show up as physical abuse, sexual abuse, bullying, and many others. Recognising these behaviours will also assist you in creating awareness that there could be anger being displaced.

Guilt helps you to correct your conduct with others and with yourself through forgiveness. You may experience guilt as a result of wrongdoing, real or imagined or imposed. However, when you experience prolonged guilt that does not lead to taking a positive action to amend the situation and free yourself from guilt, then you flow back on yourself. Are there people to whom you should say, "I am sorry"? If so, what is stopping you? Usually, people would prefer to suffer from unhealthy, prolonged guilt, because they are too proud to say they are sorry. Their egos prevent their own well-being. Sometimes people feel guilty over things they have no control over, like death. They may think they did not do enough for their loved one; hence, the loved one died. They take responsibility for something they cannot change.

You can transform your life moving forward by learning from what happened, to become a better person in the now. Ask yourself questions such as, "What could I do to prevent what makes me feel guilty so that it does not happen again?" You can get back to flow. Feeling guilty may result in blaming others or doing what you do not want to do, to compensate for your guilt without necessarily addressing it. Asking for forgiveness or forgiving yourself will help you get back in the flow. Remember that forgiveness helps you, not the other person, to get back to your divine state.

Shame is a subtle emotion, resulting from a sense of inadequacy, unworthiness, or feeling inferior. Like guilt, shame can be real, imagined, or imposed. And because it is a concealed emotion, most people are not aware of it when it shows up. You can see it, however, in their behaviors: low self-esteem, low self-confidence or self-belief, shyness, self-criticism, addiction and compulsive behaviors. We all experience genuine shame when we do not live up to our standards, but it should flow through. If it is prolonged, we flow back on ourselves. False or imposed shame can result from others, when we believe we have not lived up to their standards. Imposed shame is normally toxic in kids, who cannot rationalize, choose, or change their situation. If others make them feel inadequate, this feeling of shame, if not addressed, can get into their adult lives. Shame can be created by the words others use, such as "You are stupid, (silly, dumb)"; "What is wrong with you?"; "You have not done anything significant; you are not as good as so-and-so": or "You will never amount anything," just to mention a few.

Shame can also cause a feeling of anger, so that we become aggressive with anyone who triggers the feeling of shame. In relationships, especially husband and wife, when someone has genuine shame or does not meet his/her standards as a parent or spouse, he/she may turn to addiction, alcoholism, or even reduce the self-esteem of their loved ones—that is, their children and spouse—by blaming or attacking them. Then the children and spouse will experience imposed shame. The difference between shame and guilt is that shame says, "I am wrong as a person," and guilt says, "I have done something wrong." Shame is more destructive because of its concealed nature. You will feel you are wrong as a person, and most of the time, you will keep what makes you feel ashamed a secret; hence, there is a continuous flow back on yourself. If you have experienced shame for a long time, you may not consciously realize where it comes from if you do not revisit your life journey to diagnose or check its source, deal with it, or talk about it with someone. If you experience self-esteem and confidence issues, diagnose the concealed emotion of shame that makes you believe there is something wrong with you as a person. Remember that you are more than how you look, and no matter what you have done or not done, you deserve to be loved.

Grief is a feeling we experience when we lose someone or something we love. It can be a relationship, a person, a job, or a pet. Grieving is a natural process to healing. However, some people never heal from loss, and when that happens, they flow back on themselves. The amount of time spent grieving differs from one person to the next, but the awareness that you can heal as soon as you choose to do so—and that is your choice—is important. Prolonged or excessive grief can be harmful. Grief can also give rise to feelings of deep hurt, disappointment, disproval, depression, anger, and even fear. Loss is change; how you deal with change affects the length of your grieving period. Grief can lead to loneliness if not dealt with as you close out possible relationships.

Loathing is a feeling of intense hate for someone or something. Some people have someone they hate, and they wish that person dead. They may have killed that person in their own heads. When this happens, you flow back on yourself, because each time you see, hear, or think about this person or thing, you trigger a life-response mechanism in your body as if you are in danger, releasing the stress hormones. The language we use also triggers strong feelings. Most people say things like, "I hate my job" or "I hate so-and-so," instead of saying "I have a feeling of hate toward so-and-so," which tones down the intensity of the emotion. Loathing is an expression of disgust, when someone or something threatens our value system. The awareness that people live their own values, not yours, is critical to manage loathing. Looking at the options you have which can either be to go where your values are supported or live out your values, that is find ways to live out your values instead of getting stuck in trying to make someone else live your values.

I remember in one training session, a gentleman said, "I hate my father for not paying for my tertiary education, as he had promised, and for not looking after me as I grew up." While the reason might seem genuine to warrant those feelings, he is the one who is stuck and feeling drained. In fact, he slept through most of the training. I suspect that the intense hurt and hate he experienced was like a hole in the obstruction, sucking energy and keeping him stuck.

Insecurity is a feeling triggered by a sense of vulnerability or inferiority. Insecurity shows we are flowing back on ourselves by imagining what could happen, as a result of what we know has happened. Shame or grief can give rise to insecurity when we perceive ourselves as unstable in relationships, such as with money, loved ones, spiritually, or work. We will then have a sense of uneasiness or nervousness, and there may be excessive occurrences clumsiness, such as spilling water or dropping forks at dinner tables. Insecurity can give rise to arrogance, withdrawal, shyness, anxiety, and paranoia. Insecurity can be triggered by issues that have not been resolved from past relationships. Insecurity can cause loneliness, as some people avoid engaging because of the fear of being hurt or that someone might become controlling. Insecurity can also be created by a challenging childhood or abusive relationship. It's always a challenges to build security from the outside in. Security has to start from inside.

How stable are you as a person who is creating self-assurance? You only can be financially secure, for example, if you strongly believe that you have the ability to make money anytime you want to, instead of focusing on how much you have, as this may be affected by external forces, such as economic downturn or loss of a business or a job. But the self-belief that your internal forces—your resourcefulness—can turn the economy up, can create another business, can start again, or can find another job gives you not only resiliency and hope but certainty, security, and self-assurance. If you feel safe on the inside, you can do what it takes to feel safe on the outside without threatening yourself or others. Traps of insecurity include assuming what others maybe be thinking and focusing on the negative. So instead of thinking for others, find out what they are thinking, and focus on what is going well or what could go well.

Regret is a feeling of dissatisfaction from one's choices. We all experience regret because we make choices daily. We live in a world full of choices—some choices give us the outcomes we want and some do not. We can regret our actions or inactions, hence blaming ourselves for doing or not doing. Again, regret focuses on the negative, where we looks at "if only," and it triggers sadness, disappointment, and blame. Like any rapid on the river, you can pass through regret, learn from what happens, and keep moving forward. It should not arrest your development or derail you. When you have a continuous feeling of regret, you flow back on yourself, and the challenge is that no matter how much you may want to do over the rapids in your life, or turn back and relive again, what's done is done. Learn from it, and find your place back in the current and flow forward. If you still have an opportunity to do what you did not do, then do it. If not, focus on the good in your life as a result of that same choice.

I have passed over many rapids of regret. One of the few regrets that I have had to deal with, is that I did not spend more time with my mother in her last days, after she struggled with Alzheimer's for five years. The lesson I learned is that we never know how long we will have our loved ones with us. We should do our best to spend quality time with them. The other regret I have had is meeting the man who became the father of my son, which led to challenging single parenting for a few years. I learned, however, that what seemed like an unfortunate event had to happen. Otherwise, I wouldn't have been blessed with the handsome, intelligent, adorable, most giving boy who is my son. Nothing is one-sided. If we focus on the negative and do not learn from our experiences, we will get stuck.

Fear is the feeling that comes from a perceived threat, real or imagined. Any negative emotion we experience stems from some form of fear. Remember, we are born with two basic fears, and we learn all the other fears we experience. Most fears are irrational. They disrupt our energy system, yet they are not real threats; they are just the stories we tell ourselves. Fear is an evolutionary and strong emotion that can lead to inaction or constructive or destructive action. Exploring our fears helps us to learn from them and to give us courage to face those fears.

When you experience feelings of fear, what are you focusing on? Paralyzing fear focuses on the negative. If your fears paralyze you from taking action or result in destructive behaviors, you are flowing back on yourself.

Worry or Depression

If you are depressed, you are living in the past. If you are anxious, you are living in the future. If you are at peace, you are living in the present.

—Lao Tzu

Worry and depression are states of being that occur due to dominant negative emotions, like fear, grief, shame, regret, anger, or loathing. Worrying is an obstruction and an energy-sucker that drains you and takes energy away from you, disabling you changing what you are afraid might happen, which is causing the worry. There is a belief that if I do not worry, it means I do not care; hence, most of us get stuck in worry to show that we worry about the way things are. On the other hand, depression is going back to a past event, replaying the scenes, and triggering the emotions you felt when it happened. Continuous release of the negatively charged emotion into your bloodstream makes your body feel out of balance and depressed. When you find yourself in any of these states, you need to ask yourself, "What could I do now to give me the results I want?"

An important aspect is the awareness of what you focus on and where you spend most of your time—in the future, the past, or the present. Your focus will determine your dominant state: worry, depression, or flow. You need the ability to stop when you are aware of thoughts or emotions of worry, and observe what is triggering them. Then shift the thought pattern or emotional pattern, using either the questioning technique or any emotional freedom technique. Allow emotions to come and go. Most often, we are having an emotional response to the situation, as opposed to the situation doing anything to us

Lesson 8

Recharge

Take time to recharge your batteries. It's hard to see where you're going when your lights are dim.
—Robert H. Conelly

As we sailed down the river on the calmer waters, we shared a drink of water and some cookies and pineapples. Those who could swim took a refreshing swim, just to revitalize them. The refreshments were planned and deliberate, and for some, a jump in the water was needed.

Sometimes, people suffer from a pressure stroke. They push themselves too much without taking a break—a break from thinking, just silencing your mind from the constant chatter; a break from your work; a break from your relationships to find and connect with yourself. Even someone who is doing what they are passionate about burn out if recharging his or her batteries is not deliberate. We have energy myths that prevent us from thinking about energy management. Neville Mandy, in her book *No More Illness*, says, "Nobody ever questions the fact that we must feed our horses balanced rations, that we must correctly fertilize our plants, and that we must give octane fuel to our cars. Yet, strangely, many people seem to have extreme difficulty in understanding that bodies have the same uncompromising energy requirements as do horses, plants and motor vehicles."

How often do you think about managing your energy? Energy comes from our body, mind, emotions, and spirit. When we do not have enough energy, we feel overwhelmed, stressed, and anxious. When we are anxious or stressed, the alarm bells go off, signaling danger. The amygdala, which does not know whether the perceived threat is real or imagined, triggers the release of cortisol, a stress hormone.

> *When cortisol levels are high, working memory is reduced, distractibility is increased, information processing is reduced, emotional reactivity is heightened.*
> —Daniel Goleman

We then become reactionary and lose control of our lives and our relationships. Most of us are pressured with trying to achieve so much or being stuck in the busy-ness of the day. Let's explore a few energy-management techniques you could use to recharge. You already may be doing some of the things; the important thing is intentionality—knowing why you are doing it.

Me Time

Taking "me time" is a useful tool to break out of the routine and ease the mounting pressure from everyday demands. This helps you to slow down and have self-focus and introspection, connecting with your inner world. Focus is a key tool for success, and when you can focus intentionally, that shows awareness. Taking me time helps to reflect on what you want to do and how you want to carry yourself as a person, instead of going on auto-pilot. This is an opportunity to look within—bear in mind that the only journey is the journey within. Check if you are living out your values. If you are not, you are probably drained, unfulfilled, or frustrated. You need to create time to connect with yourself, check your states, your mood, your dominant emotions, and your pace in achieving your goals. Me time assists with self-observation. Me time is an energizer that allows you to acknowledge and honor yourself. During me time, you can also question your beliefs, your thoughts, and your states or emotions, and transform them. You can replace your regrets with dreams and goals, and look for lessons in your experience. Me time has to be deliberately planned into your schedule to design, structure or restructure your life, and refocus or take off focus for a while. You need time to check if you are focusing on the major or minor things in your life. Have a conversation with yourself that is directed. This your time of power.

Meditation and/or Prayer

Meditation is a tool to silence and calm your mind, connect with your spirit, and recharge. Prayer invokes your spiritual energy. Nick Vujicic, Australian Christian evangelist and motivational speaker recently noted that the acronym FAITH stands for "full assurance in the heart." When you pray or meditate, you go inside, in spirit and heart, to find assurance there. Going on the inside is a way to recharge and temporarily block out the pressure around you of what needs to get done. Prayer or meditation strengthen you from within or help to tap into the power within. Remarkable insights, creativity and a renewed mind, confidence, and intrinsic motivation are revived by a calm mind.

Tapping

Another tool to help recharge is tapping, or emotional freedom technique (EFT). Our emotions are energy that drive our action or inaction, and they are either positively charged or negatively charged. Negatively charged emotions cause a disruption in our bodies' energy flow system. This disruption can cause us to engage in the fight or flight for survival, as we no longer have the healthy emotions, positive energy, or clear thinking to take the appropriate action to resolve the challenge.

Tapping is sometimes called "acupuncture without needles"; it follows the meridian points. From Wikipedia, a meridian point is connected point across the anatomy, which affect a specific organ or other part of the body. Stimulating acupressure points has been found to cause blood-flow changes to the amygdala and areas in the brain that relate to mood, pain, and cravings. Hence, it helps to clear the body's energy system of the pressure of negatively charged emotions. When blood flow is reduced to the amygdala, endorphins—the feel-good hormones—increase, breaking the thought/memory and emotional reaction. This method is freely available for us to use to reduce the negative emotional patterns and to recharge.

To start with meridian tapping, follow the sequence and the tapping points below:

- To start the process, think of an issue, event, or person that triggers a negative emotional reaction. Then think of a setup phrase, based on the emotion you are feeling and the psychological reversal you want to make. For example, even though I feel stressed, I deeply and completely love, honor, and accept myself. Or even though I am anxious about a business presentation, I deeply and completely love, accept, and honor myself. The reasoning behind making the reversal is that each time we experience a negative emotion, there is an element of self-resentment, self-poisoning, or self-denial. We release negatively charged electro-chemical signals into our bloodstreams, and that does not show self-love. Hence, we have to remind ourselves that we still love and respect ourselves, which is our bodies and our souls. This is a setup statement.
- Rate the intensity of the emotional charge on a scale of one to ten, with one not really being an issue, and ten being a big problem or intense.
- Repeat the setup statement loudly enough for you to hear yourself as you tap three times on the Karate Chop (see diagram below).
- Then you will tap using a reminder phrase on top of the head, top of the eye, side of the eye, under the eye, under

the nose, under the chin, collarbone, and under the arm. The reminder statement is the issue you are dealing with, for example "this stress in my head or wherever the tension is", tapping the 9 acupressure points 10 times.

- You can tap with either the left or the right hand. Alternatively, you can use both hands to tap each side.
- Don't tap hard; it should not be uncomfortable.

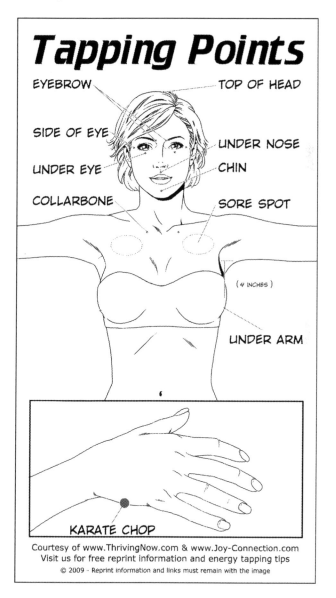

Tapping Points

EYEBROW   TOP OF HEAD

SIDE OF EYE   UNDER NOSE

UNDER EYE   CHIN

COLLARBONE   SORE SPOT

(4 INCHES)

UNDER ARM

KARATE CHOP

Courtesy of www.ThrivingNow.com & www.Joy-Connection.com
Visit us for free reprint information and energy tapping tips
© 2009 - Reprint information and links must remain with the image

Exercise

Exercise can assist us in releasing negative energy that may accumulate in our bodies. Exercise stimulates lymph drainage when sweating, that is assisting to release the negative energy or stress hormones that would have accumulated forming lymph nodes. Exercise should form part of our day routine. Exercise can mean time at the gym, aerobics, running, or anything that gets your body moving to release negatively charged signals in your body. Think about it: your boss screams at you at work, and your survival instincts are triggered, and you release the stress hormones cortisol and adrenaline for action. Most of the time, you will not fight your boss, so what happens to the stress hormones that are released? If you keep replaying the scene by telling yourself a story about what happened, you may spend the day flowing back on yourself, releasing more stress hormones. By the end of the day, you will have accumulated pressure that further stimulates the amygdala. When you get home, and your children or spouse try to get your attention, you may snap because you are already irritable from the mounting pressure of the day. Exercise such as tapping helps to stimulate the flow of blood throughout your body, and that helps you to recharge.

Eating for Health Energy

While I am not a nutritionist, I know that certain foods we eat can leave us feeling like crap. For example, when I take fizzy drinks, I get that two-minute elation, but that is followed by days of suffering, feeling sick, with a roller coaster of emotions that come with feeling unwell. Eating sugar gives that temporary energy boost, but then it drops after a few hours, if not minutes. Eating often is seen as routine or a pattern—we eat, for example, because it is lunchtime or suppertime. There is no intentionality as to the energy levels required or how we want to feel after eating this food. To recharge we also need to be conscious of what we eat, when we eat it, and why we eat it. A lot of diseases come as a result of a poor or unmonitored diet. Get more information on foods that boost your physical energy as well as your emotional energy.

Detoxification and Rehydration

When your body is bloated, it is energy draining, and you start feeling myriad negative emotions. Detoxification helps to flush out impurities from the body. There are several ways to detox, including massage, fasting, and flushing bowels. If you have gone for a massage, you may have been told that you have swollen lymph nodes, this shows the accumulation of stress and if left unattended it is energy draining and that can also result in illness.

Water is an external and internal cleanser. Because our bodies are about 65 percent water, we need to keep rehydrating. Our organs and brains need water to function normally. With an increased heart rate and cortisol in your bloodstream during stressful periods, you will lose water in your body. Hence, you need to drink more water. Keeping hydrated can lower your stress levels and assist you in keeping away from the vicious cycle of stress dehydration. Drinking water improves your emotional state and helps you to recharge.

Restorative Sleep

Sleeping has an emotional function as well as a physiology function. Research has shown that the dream state of sleep assists in sorting out deep-seated emotional issues and enhances memory, while the physiological function is rest. Sleep deprivation affects our mood states, attention, memory, and consequently, behavior. Lack of restorative sleep causes fatigue, and fatigue causes stress. Prolonged states of stress and fatigue can leave you feeling irritable and easily triggered. Negative emotions have adverse effects on restorative sleep, as any unresolved emotions may show up in your dream world, affecting your sleep quality. One hour of sleep before midnight is worth two hours of sleep after midnight, so sleeping early can help you recharge. Our bodies need rest to recharge, so take time to intentionally sleep well with the awareness that lack of it affects your mood.

Go Back to Nature

The first human beings God created lived in a garden, which is nature. Have you ever wondered why? My opinion is that everything we need is in nature, and if we go back to it, deliberately stepping out of our busy schedules and the chaos of the city, we can find and connect with the peace within. A day at the river left me feeling calm, soothed, and inspired. Unplugging and going back to nature boosts creativity, so deliberately create time to go back to nature.

Gadget-Free Day

We are run by our gadgets, and most of the time we are totally distracted, not paying attention to our surroundings or our relationships. You might see a family at a dinner table, each on a mobile phone, iPad moving from one social media to the next, bombarded by lots of information but totally distracted, as Daniel Goleman puts it. This results in us neglecting ourselves and others. Taking a day unplugged—100 percent gadget-free—gives your brain a clear, calming effect that can boost creativity and focus. Getting addicted to e-mails and commitments is like piling up pebbles in your brain. If you obsess over them, they become big rocks that can cause big rapids and start flowing back on yourself. Give yourself frequent breaks from the pebbles of your life. Switch off constant interruption and focus on relationships; positive relationships are magnifiers of positive emotions.

Learn to Ask for What You Want

It can be draining to know what you want, know who has it and who potentially could give it but to not know how to ask for it. You go through emotions of fear—"What if the person does not give it to me?"—and pride will follow—"I would rather not be rejected." But you are anxious because you want something from someone who has it, yet you are afraid and too proud to ask for it. You are stuck. To get back to flow, learn to ask for what you want in your relationships, without being manipulative, expecting a yes or a no. If someone says yes, you will be recharged and feel happy; and if he or she says no, look for other avenues to get what you want, instead of being stuck. Asking for what you want is liberating and rejuvenating.

Know When to Change Action to Get Rid of Energy Vampires

Sometimes we give power to external conditions by persisting with the same action and producing the results we do not want. This can get us stuck. Choosing a different course of action is energizing. Do not tolerate being stuck in the same pattern forever. It is stagnating, and when you are stagnant, you are not necessarily recharged. Always be aware of your emotional patterns and key defense mechanisms, such as repression, reaction formation, and displacement. Repression is when one blocks unpleasant emotional experiences that bring anxiety from their conscious mind, however while this helps one cope, it makes one emotionally inaccessible to others. Reaction formation is also a coping mechanism where expresses the contrast of what they are feeling and displacement is transferring your emotions These patterns are draining, and you set up a trap for yourself. Pay attention and notice if these impulses arise. Stop, observe, and shift your emotions, pattern, or behavior. Lack of self-confidence and low self-esteem are energy vampires. Diagnose their root cause, and deal with the issues surrounding how they showed up in your life, remembering that you are not born with them.

Make Gratitude a Discipline

> *Gratitude unlocks the fullness of life. It turns what we have into enough, and more. It turns denial into acceptance, chaos to order, and confusion to clarity. It can turn a meal into a feast, a house into a home, a stranger into a friend.*
> —Melody Beattie

Happiness for a grateful person is automatic, You cannot be grateful and sad at the same time. We live in a world bombarded with constant negative news, not because there is no good happening but because the majority of people focus on the negative. To find your place back in the current and flow, make a gratitude ritual. Find three things daily to be thankful for in your life. If you say there is nothing, you are not being truthful. Bitching, moaning, and whining are energy drainers. Authentic appreciation of your relationships, your resources (both natural and those you have built), the good times you have had, and your successes boosts your energy levels. Everything around you is a gift or a stepping stone to your next level. Nothing is one-sided, and no matter what challenges you may face, there is always something to be thankful for. Gratitude helps you with self-control, directing your focus to the positive rather than concentrating on the negative.

Lesson 9

Flow on Purpose and Live

There is no passion to be found playing small—in settling
for a life that is less than the one you are capable of living.
—Nelson Mandela

After the river-raft adventure, which I did with very little awareness, I began reading and searching for the history of the Nile. I discovered that the river Nile flows across about eleven countries— Ethiopia, Eritrea, Sudan, Egypt, Uganda, Democratic Republic of the Congo, Kenya, Tanzania, Rwanda, Burundi, and South Sudan. The Nile River touches many lives before it contributes to the bigger waters of the Mediterranean Sea. River Nile flows on purpose, to contribute to the universe and in harmony with its natural laws.

When I looked back, I realized that the Nile River makes a statement—that at the river, you can experience tranquility, have fun and be happy, refresh, recharge, connect, and navigate as you interact with its purpose. River Nile makes a statement about its purpose as it flows through the eleven countries, touching lives significantly in small and big ways.

Life on the river is not about what you do, how you look, or where you live. It is about who you are, how much fun you're having, and the connections you make with nature, with yourself, and with the people who surround you.

Mavis Mazhura

What Is Your Contribution?

A lot has been written on the subject of purpose, but this discussion aims to help you see how living your purpose enhances your emotional stability. Discovering your purpose and contribution to humanity assists you in being fulfilled when you live it out. What makes you feel fulfilled? When you are fulfilled inside, you can give yourself better to other people; you show up as your best when you live on purpose. My opinion is that your purpose is the first love of your life—the reason you exist and the essence of your personality. Find love—the first love of your life—and live it. When you serve love and not your fears, you will flow and engage with others in a more meaningful way.

Most people wonder what their purpose is and feel that purpose has to be big. I think we cannot all be Nelson Mandela or Martin Luther King Jr., but we all can contribute in some way. Some of us may be mothers, by default or by nature, but not by a calling or as a purpose. There are people who have been called to be mothers and do it very well; no one else can replicate it. However, some of us become better mothers, because we are living our purpose. For example, I see my purpose as teaching. I want to dedicate my life to teaching and raising human awareness and consciousness. When I come back home from a teaching day, I am happy, and I can connect with my children from a place of wellness and fulfillment, and that makes me a better mother.

When you contribute from a place of awareness that it is the reason you exist, it boosts your confidence and gives you a clearer sense of direction. If someone came to you and said, "Chose your job, and I will pay you for it," would you still carry on doing what you are currently doing? If not, what would you do? If you had to write your own job description, what would you write? What do you love to do?

The challenge with living out your purpose is that most people will also say they have no time to do it, that they have to earn a living or have no money to pursue their dreams. I always ask, "How is what you are currently doing on the way and not in the way?" When see what you are currently doing as on the way, it ceases to be a barrier to living out your purpose; it becomes an activator. Think about it: how would you feel if you dedicated at least thirty minutes of your twenty-four hours each day to doing something that is the love of your life? What would you like to be remembered for? What values and what strengths? When you know your contribution, you can connect with others with intention or in a purposeful way.

Finding the Sanctuary Within

> *Men, like nails, lose their usefulness when they lose direction and begin to bend.*
> —Walter Savage Landor

Discovering your purpose connects you with the sanctuary within, a direction that cannot be easily swayed by external forces. When you have discovered your purpose, it is not easy to be sidetracked or distracted. If does happen, it is easy to go back to it. When you are not fulfilled due to not living out your purpose, it is easy to feel frustrated and/or to frustrate others in the process. Because you are unwell inside yourself, you are not being authentic. When some people are frustrated by not being authentic to themselves or to their God-given purposes, they might seek sedatives or anesthetics to temporarily soothe themselves from feeling unwell. They lose focus on their usefulness and begin to bend, engaging in self-sabotaging behaviors, such as alcoholism, womanizing, making others responsible for their happiness, complaining, being a seductress, or simply being idle. These behaviors also perpetuate a feeling of false fulfillment and unhappiness that hurts themselves and others.

If you do not pursue something worthwhile, you will pursue something worthless. People pursue different things in search of happiness. Some pursue money, some pursue marriage, and some pursue children, only to discover that none of the things they pursed gives them that sense of peace. This is because they have not pursued their true mission. I believe when you pursue your purpose, you other desires will ultimately be added on and even if they were not it would not be an issue for you. When you limit what you are capable of or who you truly are, that drains energy out of your being.

Journey to Self-Exploration

> *The only journey is the one within.*
> —Rainer Maria Rilke

> *And you? When will you begin that long journey into yourself?*
> —Rumi

Discovering and living your purpose gets you on a journey within, a journey to self-discovery. On this journey, you will continually discover yourself, and you are in a place where it is no longer about others' influences. Purpose provides you with a compass to go in and out. When you are on a journey to self-exploration, you never stop learning about yourself, and as you learn about yourself, you develop emotional muscles that enhance flow, such as self-love, self-respect, self-appreciation, self-compassion, patience, delayed gratification, and contentment. This journey helps you appreciate the journey that came before and look forward to the journey ahead, getting deeper within yourself and building a stronger self-connection. As you build a stronger self-connection, you will be able to connect with others in a special way, a way that makes them feel valued. When you know yourself, it will be easier to understand others.

Where do you live internally? Are your dominant emotions about what you love or what you do not love? Is it about your purpose, or is it about others or your material requirements? Have you mastered your internal world?

Lesson 10

Celebrate the Unsung Hero inside You

I think a hero is an ordinary individual who finds strength
to persevere and endure, in spite of overwhelming obstacles.
—Christopher Reeve

As we got to the end of our river-raft journey and pulled off the river, we celebrated for accomplishing our journey. We drank, ate, sang, and connected with each other, being thankful for the journey. We parted, wishing each other well, and carried on with our individual journeys.

Thank You to You

Let gratitude be the pillow upon which you kneel to say
your nightly prayer.
—Maya Angelou

When you look at your journey, are you brave enough to say thank you to you for having been there for you when no one else understood how you felt; thank you to all who made the journey what it is today; thank you to God for being there, even when you did not feel His presence; thank you that you are still here? And when you look at where you are now and the challenges you continue to conquer on your journey, can you see that unsung hero inside you?

We forget to celebrate the good times and our accomplishments, as we are always pressured to go to the next level of achievement and don't pay attention to how our story is unfolding. Celebrating and being thankful is an energizer; it creates flow of energy back to you, making you see what you are capable of doing and silencing voices that say you cannot win—voices of fear, fatigue, and low self-concept. When you are thankful, it is possible to have your ideals.

Look back and see what you have been through. It is always important to continue to look forward, but from time to time, it is important to look back and see what you have been through. Looking back delivers some perspective, much satisfaction, and certain comfort in knowing you have navigated rough waters successfully. It gives you confidence for what is ahead.

Unsung heroes are ordinary people like you and me—people who have walked journeys that, when we trace the path, the feelings we experience are the ones only tears can express and appreciate what courage, strength, passion, love, hope and faith we had. But had we not walked those journeys, we would have never known what key strengths we possess. Our stories from where we have been do not change. We can change the way we look at them and the meaning we give them, but they have shaped us and make us who we are. Hence, we need to acknowledge and celebrate the victories won and lessons learned. Any unacknowledged, denied, or suppressed stories can have adverse effects in our lives. As we suppress the story, we also suppress the emotions that come up in each episode of the story. We may be locked in emotional bondage.

We overcame—that was our then. And we are here *now*. What is your story? Become conversant with it, and get insights from it.

Celebrating helps us to appreciate life. Most of our regrets emanate from our not having appreciated our relationships, not having spent more time with ourselves and others. We are there but not really there. Everyone is on a journey and has a story about that journey. Celebrate the hero in others.

At the End of the Journey

Coming to the end of the journey is a change. I have lost people dear to me; maybe you have too. My sister, my mother, and my brothers—their journey came to an end, and they left. But like most people, when I experienced loss, grief hit hard. My little brother, who was first to go, was too young—just a university student. He did not deserve to die. That is how I felt at the time. But I know now that every journey will come to an end, and when it does, we have to say good-bye and carry on with our journey until it comes to an end. I realize that it is important to let others know what my journey is all about or what I desire to accomplish with my purpose. Then, when I come to the end of my journey, people can celebrate and shed tears of appreciation that I came, and they will be thankful that I managed to accomplish certain things on my journey. They can celebrate at the end of my journey, looking back at the accomplishments and the battles fought—some won, and some with lessons learned.

Choose celebration at the end of any journey—life, career, health, financial, mental, spiritual, family, and social.

Appendix

Pick your core value or characteristic. What is most important to you?

- Independence/freedom
- Dependable or dependence
- Security
- Flexibility
- Productivity/getting things done
- Financial freedom
- Reliability
- Loyalty
- Authenticity
- Humility
- Discernment
- Holism
- Wisdom
- Health
- Family
- Food
- Self-expression
- Friends
- Relationships
- Emotional wellness
- Lifestyle
- Personal growth
- Contribution
- Purpose of life

- Generosity
- Order
- Wealth
- Work
- Fame
- Peace of mind
- Committed
- Open-minded
- Consistent
- Respect
- Spiritual
- Fulfillment
- Work
- Life
- Travel
- Sense of accomplishment
- Honest
- Efficient
- Innovative
- Creative
- Humor/happiness
- Fun-loving
- Adventurous
- Motivated
- Positive
- Optimistic
- Inspiring
- Passionate
- Respectful
- Athletic
- Fit
- Courageous
- Educated
- Respected
- Loving
- Nurturing

- Empowerment
- Risk taking
- Thoughtfulness
- Connection
- Variety
- Significance
- Accepted
- Loved
- Known

Self-Image

Put this list someplace where you can see it, and remind yourself regularly of all your good qualities.

I am …

- Adaptable
- Adventurous
- Affectionate
- Ambitious
- Artistic
- Assertive
- Broad-minded
- Capable
- Caring
- Charming
- Cheerful
- Clearheaded
- Clever
- Compassionate
- Competent
- Confident
- Conscientious
- Considerate

- Courageous
- Creative
- Dependable
- Determined
- Devoted
- Dynamic
- Easygoing
- Efficient
- Energetic
- Enterprising
- Enthusiastic
- Fair
- Faithful
- Flexible
- Friendly
- Funny
- Generous
- Gentle
- Glad
- Good-natured
- Happy
- Helpful
- Honest
- Hopeful
- Idealistic
- Imaginative
- Independent
- Industrious
- Intelligent
- Inventive
- Kind
- Likable
- Logical
- Lovable
- Mature
- Merry

- Modest
- Natural
- Neat
- Nonjudgmental
- Nurturing
- Open-minded
- Optimistic
- Organized
- Original
- Outgoing
- Patient
- Peaceful
- Persevering
- Persistent
- Pleasant
- Polite
- Positive
- Practical
- Precise
- Progressive
- Punctual
- Rational
- Realistic
- Reasonable
- Reflective
- Relaxed
- Reliable
- Resourceful
- Responsible
- Robust
- Sexy
- Sincere
- Sociable
- Spontaneous
- Spunky
- Stable

- Strong
- Tactful
- Talented
- Tenacious
- Thorough
- Tolerant
- Trusting
- Trustworthy
- Truthful
- Understanding
- Unique
- Versatile
- Warm
- Witty
- Zany

Positive Traits/Strengths

- Adaptable
- Articulate
- Artistic
- Athletic
- Clever
- A communicator
- Confident
- Dexterous
- Diplomatic
- Energetic
- Entertaining
- Generous
- Grateful
- Hardworking
- Imaginative
- Insightful
- Intelligent

- Kind
- A leader
- Open-minded
- Optimistic
- A philosopher
- Practical
- Sincere

Negative Traits/Weaknesses

- Antisocial
- Compulsive
- Dishonest
- Disorganized
- Distrustful
- Egotistical
- Excessive
- Fearful
- Impulsive
- Inflexible
- Insecure
- Intolerant
- Irresponsible
- Narrow-minded
- Obsessive
- Pessimistic
- Alcohol or drug dependent
- Pretentious
- Prideful
- Procrastinator
- Reactive
- Selfish
- Prejudiced
- Tedious
- Unaware

- Uncharitable
- Uncommitted
- Unenthusiastic
- Ungrateful
- Unmotivated
- Unreliable
- Vague

Become a better and more powerful you

in the next 6 Weeks

than you have been in the

Past 6 Months

With the 6 Week "Emotional Mastery " Mentoring Program

You will receive one-on-one sessions for 6 weeks taking you through a proven process will help you:

- Develop your Emotional Literacy and become more **Self-aware**
- Make informed **decisions**
- Set **emotional boundaries and goals**
- Live in **integrity** with your **values**
- Appreciate your **relationships** and your **purpose**
- Become a more **creative and healthier you**

Visit www.eMotions4Success.com for more programmes